The Very Special Raspberry Cookbook

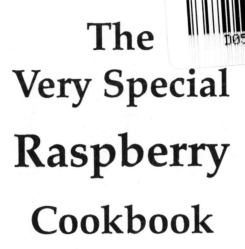

benefitting
Carrie Tingley Hospital Foundation
and
Very Special Arts New Mexico

Albuquerque, New Mexico

The Very Special Raspberry Cookbook
Copyright 1993
The Very Special Raspberry Cookbook Committee
Albuquerque, NM

First Printing 1993,   5,300 copies
Second Printing 1995,   5,000 copies

ISBN: 0-9646119-0-2

Printed in the USA by

WIMMER
The Wimmer Companies, Inc.
Memphis • Dallas

Table of Contents

Very Special Arts New Mexico

Carrie Tingley Hospital

It All Started With Raspberries

Acknowledgements

About the Cover Artist

To Order Cover Art Prints

Index

Index Additions

VERY SPECIAL ARTS
NEW MEXICO

The mission of Very Special Arts New Mexico is to demonstrate the value of the arts in the lives of children and adults with disabilities.

The mission is accomplished by developing demonstration models in the Albuquerque area and encouraging accessible visual and performing arts programs and related services in school and community settings throughout New Mexico. These programs and services strive to be reflective of and value all cultures and to assist persons with disabilities in achieving fair and equitable participation in community cultural life.

VSA NM achieves its mission through the operation of a state office in Albuquerque and *VSA: Arts Access New Mexico*, a network of arts accessibility advocates in communities around New Mexico. Statewide outreach and demonstration efforts are coordinated through the Albuquerque office. The programs and services offered include **Arts Accessibility Initiatives**, which develop resources to support arts programming for, by and with individuals with disabilities; **Very Special Arts Festivals and Special Events**; The **BUEN VIAJE DANCERS**, a touring performance group; and the **ENABLED Arts Center**, a studio arts program for youth and adults with disabilities. In pursuing this mission, VSA NM works toward the day when its goals are achieved and its special services are no longer needed.

VSA NM is an accredited state program of Very Special Arts, an international organization dedicated to providing arts programs for persons with disabilities and an educational affiliate of The John F. Kennedy Center for the Performing Arts.

Very Special Arts New Mexico can be contacted at P.O. Box 7784, Albuquerque, New Mexico, 87194, 505/245-8545.

VERY
SPECIAL
ARTS
NEW MEXICO

Enriching the lives of people with disabilities

CARRIE TINGLEY HOSPITAL

The University of New Mexico

Carrie Tingley Hospital, part of the Medical Center of the University of New Mexico, provides responsive, caring and coordinated health care services to New Mexico's children, adolescents, and young adults up to the age of 21 who have chronic impairments and who require long-term inpatient and outpatient medical or orthopedic surgical care or treatment. Such services are directed to the whole child and family. Carrie Tingley Hospital seeks to achieve maximum habilitation of the patient and integrate the patient into the community as a productive citizen. It also serves in the education of orthopedic surgeons, pediatricians, and other children's health care providers while providing the highest quality medical care and engaging in scientific research.

CARRIE TINGLEY HOSPITAL FOUNDATION INC.

A separate nonprofit organization, the Carrie Tingley Hospital Foundation, raises funds to supplement the hospital's budget and to assist patients. Regular allocations are made for family transportation and lodging, patient equipment, educational seminars, and special programs. Recent special programs have included: a new cerebral palsy clinic, a dental clinic, a therapy toy lending library, and a new therapy pool.

The Foundation is administered by a volunteer Board of Trustees and a small staff, and depends upon dozens of volunteers each year to carry out its fundraising mission. The Foundation is located at the hospital, and can be contacted at 1127 University Blvd. NE, Albuquerque, New Mexico, 87102, (505) 243-6626

IT ALL STARTED
WITH RASPBERRIES

Who would imagine raspberries growing in High Desert Country? Among the many treasures of the Land of Enchantment, New Mexico, are its bountiful raspberry bushes. The first Spanish explorers called the Northern New Mexico river Mora, which means berry, for the profusion of wild raspberries they found growing along the river and in the valley. Today, the Salman Ranch, located near the Mora River, is the state's largest commercial raspberry growing operation. The Salman family has donated the raspberries for the Very Special Raspberry Festivals which benefit the University of New Mexico's Carrie Tingley Hospital Foundation and Very Special Arts New Mexico. Both groups provide services to hundreds of New Mexico young people with special needs.

The Very Special Raspberry Cookbook idea came to us naturally, after experiencing the variety of recipes served at the Raspberry Festivals. People from all parts of New Mexico helped create this cookbook by contributing their recipes, their art work, and their time spent in promotional activities. We have tried to make this a "people" book by including tidbits about our contributors.

This second edition of the Very Special Raspberry Cookbook is a tribute to raspberries, other New Mexico products, and the many volunteers who contributed to the success of the first edition - a sellout in a year! This edition has been revised and updated to include recipes from our new Governor, Lt. Governor, and Mayor of Albuquerque.

Enjoy the recipes, the tips about growing, storing, freezing, eating raspberries, and the Special Menus. Remember, most of the recipes for baked goods are adjusted for New Mexico's high altitude (5,000 ft. and above). We are proud to have developed this cookbook and hope you will get as much pleasure as we do from cooking with the Very Special Raspberry Cookbook.

The Very Special Raspberry Cookbook Committee

Bobbie Engle, Chairman
Donna Peck, Beth Rosenstein,
Barbara Schmider, Marianne Dickinson

"Thank You"
Crayons on paper
Naomi Nelson - Age 10
Patient at Carrie Tingley Hospital

ACKNOWLEDGEMENTS

Our committee members, many of whom spent countless hours on the book researching, typing, editing, testing and tasting, were all volunteers. The book exists because of their dedication and hard work.

EDITORS: Donna Peck, Beth Rosenstein

STEERING COMMITTEE: Donna Peck, Beth Rosenstein, Karen Turner, Laura Smigielski, Pam Musser

PRODUCTION & DESIGN: Marianne Dickinson

T&T (TESTERS AND TASTERS): Carolyn Hudson - chairman; Mary Lou Ashwill, Ruth Bear, Edwina Beard, Lorraine K. Beel, Alice Blackley, Cathy Bollinger, Char Brebach, Shirley Cashwell, Genevieve Chavez, Margaret Czar, Marianne Dickinson, Patte DiMonaco, Margery Dixon, Darlene Evers, Beverly Forman, Renee Grant, Kathleen Godfrey, Kathleen Howe, Sue Jackson, Sally and Hugh Kabat, Ileen Karlsson, Nancy Kilpatrick, Lela Lynes, Janet Matwiyoff, Julie McIntosh, Antje Muir, Pam Musser, Peggy Ritchie, Judith Sussman, Lorraine Tafoya, Mary Ann Twiest, Janet Weed, Joyce Weitzel

MARKETING: Laura Smigielski, Scott Alley, Margaret Czar, Ann O'Leary, Chandra Manning, Mary Montaño, Beth Rudolph

ART WORK COLLECTORS: Pam Musser, Karen Turner

COPY EDITING: Marianne Dickinson, Betsy Case, Bobbie Engle

RECIPE COLLECTORS: Joy Jeffrey, Genevieve Chavez, Janet Matwiyoff

COMPUTER GENUISES: Barbara Schmider, Bobbie Engle, Ed Dover

RASPBERRY and NEW MEXICO PRODUCE RESEARCH: Janet Matwiyoff, Jeff and David Salman, Margaret Lilley, Joy Jeffrey

TREASURER: Kitty Smith

PHOTOGRAPHY: Greg Johnston

RASPBERRY LOGO: Carolyn Kinsman

"SEED MONEY": Maggie's Raspberry Ranch

SPONSOR: American Home Furnishings

ABOUT THE COVER:
The charming woodblock print used on our cover was done by Lea Bradovich. Her woodblock prints have explored the pantheon of New Mexico's Santos as well as the medicinal plants common to the traditional healers of the Southwest. Using blocks of clear pine, Ms. Bradovich carves her images, hand-prints them, and hand-colors each one so that they are unique. She has participated in the Very Special Arts Festivals.

Menus

Untitled (Watercolor)
Teresa Pickle
Apprentice Artist at ENABLED Art Center,
Albuquerque

Menus

Dinner in the Governor's Mansion

Freshly Tossed Green Salad
* Beef Bourguignon
* Noodles with Poppy Seeds
  Green Beans with Sauteéd Almonds
  Crusty Rolls
* Schaum Torte with Fresh Raspberries

Dee and Governor Gary Johnson   *Santa Fe*

Governor Gary and Dee Johnson moved into the Governor's Mansion in 1995. This menu is one of Dee's all time favorites which she has enjoyed making for many special occasions. Both Gary and Dee are excellent cooks. The Governor, while still a young boy, did much of the cooking for his family and even taught his brothers to cook.

Beef Bourguignon

3 T. oil	1/4 tsp. thyme
2 lbs. lean cubed beef	1 3/4 c. beef broth
2 T. flour	1 3/4 c. Burgundy wine
1 tsp. salt	1 1/2 c. sliced fresh mushrooms
1/4 tsp. pepper	1 c. fresh small white onions or 1 small can

Brown meat in oil. Stir in flour, salt, pepper, and thyme. Mix well with meat, scraping the bottom of the pan. Put everything in a 3 qt. casserole. Mix broth and wine together and pour over meat. Cover and bake 325° oven for 2 1/2 hours. Add mushrooms and onions. Bake another 30 minutes. Add additional broth and wine in equal parts if needed.

Time: 3 hours
Temperature: 350°
Servings: 6

i

Noodles with Poppy Seeds

1 12 oz. pkg. wide noodles   1 T. to 2 T. poppy seeds

Prepare noodles as directed on the package. Drain and toss with poppy seeds. Serve topped with Beef Bourguignon.

Schaum Torte
with Fresh Raspberries

3 egg whites   2 to 3 pts. fresh raspberries
1/4 tsp. cream of tartar   Whipped cream or low fat yogurt
3/4 c. sugar

Beat together egg whites and cream of tartar until frothy. Gradually beat in sugar, 1 tablespoon at a time. Beat until very stiff and glossy. Bake in a 9-inch spring form pan or muffin tins, well greased, in 300° oven for 35 minutes. (May also shape on brown paper to bake.) Always make form concave so you can have a place for the raspberries. This recipe should make 10-12 individual tortes or 1 large one. They increase in size during baking. Serve with fresh raspberries and top with whipped cream or low fat yogurt.

Time: 35 minutes
Temperature: 300°
Servings: 10-12

Lieutenant Governor's Favorite Meal

* Catfish Filets
  Fresh Green Beans
  Sweet Potatoes with Marshmallow Cream
  Garden Salad or Raspberry Spinach Salad (see Index)
  Rolls and Butter
* Apple Kuchen

Deb and Lt. Governor Walter Bradley   *Clovis*

Lt. Governor Walter Bradley was inaugurated in January 1995. The Bradleys' daughter was born during that same month. What a busy way to start the year! Deb submitted this recipe because the Lt. Governor not only enjoys eating the catfish, but he's also in charge of preparing it.

♥Catfish Filets

Lemon pepper (to taste)   Seasoned salt (to taste)
Mrs. Dash (to taste)   Catfish filets (1/3 lb. per serving)
Garlic salt (to taste)

Clean filets of fish. Sprinkle above seasonings on both sides of catfish. Broil three to four minutes on each side. When they flake, they are done. Use as little or as much seasoning as you like.

Time: 6 to 8 minutes

Apple Kuchen

1/2 c. butter
1 pkg. (18 oz.) yellow cake mix
3/4 c. coconut
1/2 c. chopped pecans
1 (21 oz.) can apple pie filling

1/2 c. sugar
1 tsp. cinnamon
1 c. sour cream
2 eggs

Preheat oven to 350°.

Cut butter into yellow cake mix until crumbly. Mix in coconut and chopped nuts. Pat mixture lightly into an ungreased 13x9 inch pan, building up edges. Bake ten minutes.

Spread apple pie filling over warm crust. Mix sugar and cinnamon and sprinkle over the apple pie filling. Blend sour cream with eggs and drizzle over apples. (Topping doesn't completely cover the apples.) Bake 25 minutes.

Time: 10 minutes, then 25 minutes
Temperature: 350°
Servings: 8 to 10

"Alburquerque Turque"

* Turkey Stuffed with Chorizo and Tamale Dressing
* Red Chile Sauce
  Mashed Potatoes
  Seasonal Green Vegetable or Salad
  Freshly made rolls or flour tortillas
* Empanaditas Fritas

Mayor Martin Chavez and Margaret Aragon de Chavez   Albuquerque

Martin Chavez's term as Albuquerque's mayor began in 1994. Marty and Margaret have been married seven years and have a daughter, Martinique, who is 4 1/2 years old, and a son, Zeke who is 1 1/2 years old. They enjoy doing things together as a family, especially cooking. This menu is a holiday favorite (either Thanksgiving or Christmas) where Marty and Margaret do the cooking, Martinique helps measure and Zeke helps by tasting. Margaret says this is the most flavorful holiday turkey she has ever tasted.
Albuquerque, "The Duke City", was named for the Spanish Duke de Alburquerque and lost an "r" somewhere in the last 150 years.

Chorizo and Tamale Dressing

8 oz. chorizo (spicy Mexican
   sausage), cooked and drained
1 large onion, chopped
1/4 c. butter
2 dozen tamales, crumbled
1 recipe (8x10 pan) day old corn
   bread, crumbled

2 eggs
1 1/4 c. chicken stock
1/2 tsp. cumin
Salt and pepper to taste
12 to 16 lb. turkey

Over low heat melt 1/4 cup butter in a large pot. Lightly sauté the chopped onion. Then stir in chorizo. Crumble in the corn bread and tamales. Add remaining ingredients and mix thoroughly. Stuff the turkey with dressing and follow the roasting directions which accompany the turkey. When your turkey is finished roasting, remove the dressing and serve with the red chile sauce and turkey.

v

Red Chile Sauce

1 medium onion, chopped
1 garlic clove, crushed
Turkey giblets
Vegetable oil
45 oz. frozen or bottled red chile
 sauce (not salsa)

5 c. chicken stock
2 tsp. red chile powder
1/2 tsp. poultry seasoning
1 tsp. salt

In a large stock pot lightly sauté onion, garlic, and giblets in a small amount of oil. Add remaining ingredients and simmer the sauce for several hours while the turkey is roasting. Use the sauce to baste the turkey. This will enhance the color and flavor of the turkey. When the turkey is cooked, remove the giblets from the sauce and serve the sauce with your turkey and dressing.

Empanaditas Fritas (Fried Fruit Turnovers)

1 tsp. active dry yeast
1 1/2 c. water (105° - 115° F.)
4 c. flour
1 tsp. salt
1/4 c. shortening

Fruit filling (such as mincemeat or
 apple)
Shortening
1 T. powdered sugar (optional)

Dissolve yeast in water in a small mixing bowl. Combine flour and salt in a large mixing bowl and cut in shortening. Make a well in center of dry ingredients. Add liquid to dry ingredients and work into a dough. Knead dough until it is smooth and satiny.

Roll dough to a 1/4-inch thickness on a lightly floured board. Cut pastry into circles 3 inches in diameter. Place a spoonful of filling off center on each pastry circle. Fold pastry in half over filling and pinch edges together to seal.

Heat 2 inches of shortening in a heavy pan at medium high heat. Fry empanaditas until golden on both sides, turning only once. Drain on absorbent towels. Sprinkle empanaditas with powdered sugar, if desired.

Note: In New Mexico, empanaditas are also made with a meat filling. Both the fruit and meat empanaditas freeze well.

Total frying time: 20 to 30 minutes
Temperature: Medium-High
Servings: 6-9 dozen. Quantity will vary with size of the circles.

Dinner at the King Ranch

Raspberry Spinach Salad (see index)
* Baked Chicken Breast with Mushroom Gravy
Mashed Potatoes
Mixed Vegetables
Rolls with Butter
* Raspberry Cream Soufflé
Biscochitos
Coffee or Tea

Governor Bruce and Alice King   *Stanley*

The former Governor and Mrs. King are very supportive of the annual Raspberry Festivals. Mrs. King has been Honorary Chairman every year and has been a member of the Carrie Tingley Hospital Board.

Baked Chicken with Mushroom Gravy

2 frying chickens (about   1/2 c. butter or margarine
   1 1/2 lb. each), quartered   1 1/2 c. hot chicken broth
Paprika, salt & pepper   1 lb. fresh mushrooms
   to taste   1 c. light cream

Preheat oven to 350°.

Wash the chicken pieces and wipe dry. Sprinkle with paprika, salt and pepper. Melt the butter in a skillet. Add the chicken and sauté, turning until golden on all sides. Remove to a baking dish. Add the chicken broth. Bake, covered, in heated oven for 1 hour. Baste occasionally while cooking.

Clean mushrooms and wipe dry. If large, cut in half. When the chicken has cooked 1 hour, add the mushroom caps and cream. Continue cooking until the chicken is tender, at least 10 minutes. Serve the chicken topped with the mushrooms and sauce.

Time: 1 hour and 10 minutes
Temperature: 350°
Servings: 6 to 8

Raspberry Cream Soufflé

1 env. unflavored gelatin
1/4 c. cold water
1 (8 oz.) pkg. cream cheese
1 (10 oz.) pkg. frozen
   raspberries, thawed

2 egg whites
1 (7 oz.) jar marshmallow
   creme
1 c. heavy cream, whipped

Soften gelatin in water, stirring often, over low heat until dissolved. Combine softened cream cheese and gelatin, mixing at medium speed until well blended. Stir in raspberries. Chill until slightly thickened. Beat egg whites until soft peaks form. Gradually add marshmallow creme, beating until stiff peaks form. Fold egg white mixture and whipped cream into gelatin mixture. Wrap a 3-inch collar of foil around top of 1-quart soufflé dish. Secure with tape. Pour mixture into dish. Chill several hours or overnight. Remove foil collar before serving. Garnish with fresh raspberries.

Servings: 6 to 8

The Lunas' Favorite Supper

* Posole with Red Chile Sauce
* Red Chile Torta
* Pinto Beans
  Flour Tortillas (see index)
  Natillas(see index)

Beverly Luna and Lt. Gov. Casey Luna   *Belen*

Beverly Luna, a Carrie Tingley Hospital Foundation Board member, and her husband, former Lt. Governor Casey Luna, host an annual gala as a fund-raiser for the hospital. Beverly says this supper is Casey's favorite meal.

Posole

1 pkg. frozen posole	3 dry red chile peppers
1 med. onion, minced	3 T. red chile sauce
1 sm. pork roast	Salt to taste

Wash the posole. Place in large pot and cover with water. Add minced onion. Cover and cook over medium heat until tender. Cut up the pork roast to serving-size pieces. Place in a separate pan and cover with water. Simmer until pork is very tender, about an hour.

When the posole is done, the water will have boiled down. Add the pork roast and its water to the posole. Salt to taste and add the red chile peppers and red chile sauce to posole. Simmer for 30 minutes.

Time: 3 1/2 hours
Servings: 6 to 8

Posole in the Southwest is fresh hominy, usually found frozen, dried, or canned. Red chile peppers and sauce are optional. If there are young children eating, Beverly adds the red peppers and sauce to individual bowls. Green chile can be substituted for red chile and pork chops for pork roast.

Red Chile

RED CHILE PURÉE:

14 to 20 red chiles   2 c. water (enough to cover)

Wash and clean dry red chile pods. Take out stem and seeds. Place red chile pods on cookie sheet or large cake pan. Bake at 350° until chile pods are soft but not brown, about 1/2 hour. Put pods in blender and add water. Purée until a red, thick paste. Unused portions may be frozen.

RED CHILE SAUCE:

2 T. flour	1 1/2 c. water
2 T. oil	4 cloves garlic, crushed
1 c. chile purée	Salt to taste

Brown flour and oil together to make a roux. Add chile purée and water. Bring to a boil and simmer until consistency of gravy. Add garlic and salt. Simmer 1/2 hour more.

Red Chile Con Torta

3 eggs, separated   2 T. oil for frying
1 T. ground cracker crumbs

Add cracker crumbs to slightly-beaten egg yolks. Beat egg whites until stiff. Gently fold egg yolks into egg whites. Drop mixture by tablespoonful into a hot, greased frying pan. Brown on each side. Put on paper towel to drain. After all the patties are fried, put into Red Chile Sauce. Excellent with beans and tortillas.

Pinto Beans

3 to 4 c. dry pinto beans   3 T. oil
6 to 8 c. water   2 1/2 T. flour

Clean pinto beans, removing any rocks, bad beans and cracked beans. Wash beans in cold water until water stays clear. Put beans in large crock-pot or large pot. Fill pot to top with water. Bring to a boil, then simmer, covered, until beans are tender, stirring frequently. (Beans can be put on at night and simmered on low all night.) More water may be added during cooking time.

In a small frying pan, make a roux using oil and flour, stirring roux into the cooked beans. Stir; add salt to taste.

United States Senate
WASHINGTON, D. C.

Dinner with a Senator in Washington, D.C.

* Fiesta Cucumber Soup
* Arroz con Pollo
  Raspberry Spinach Salad (see index)
  Warm, Crusty Rolls
* Glazed Strawberry Pie

Nancy Domenici and the
Honorable Pete Domenici   *Washington, D.C.*

Senator Domenici has been representing New Mexico in the Senate since 1972. Nancy wrote that she was very excited about the project and wished us the very greatest success.

Fiesta Cucumber Soup

3 med. cucumbers, peeled,
   seeded & chunked
1 clove garlic
3 c. chicken broth (canned
   or from cubes)

3 c. light sour cream
1 T. white vinegar
2 tsp. salt

Combine cucumbers and garlic in blender. Whirl until smooth with a little chicken broth. Blend in remaining broth. Stir in sour cream. Season with white vinegar and salt. Cover and chill. Serve in small bowls. Pass around garnishes, each in different bowls or cups. Use as many or as few as you wish.

GARNISHES:
Chopped parsley
Bacon bits
Croutons
Chopped green peppers

Thinly-sliced green onions,
   including tops
Cashews, almonds or
   pecans, salted
Fresh tomatoes, diced

Servings: 8

Arroz con Pollo

1 lg. chicken, cut up in serving pieces	1/2 tsp. pepper
4 c. water, boiling	2 sprigs parsley, chopped
2 tsp. salt	1 bay leaf
1 lg. onion, chopped	1/2 tsp. saffron
2 cloves garlic, minced	2 to 4 canned pimientos, chopped
1 1/2 c. raw rice	Ground red chile, oregano, basil, or thyme (opt.)
1/2 c. olive oil	
1 tsp. paprika	

Put chicken in large pot with boiling water and 1/2 teaspoon of the salt. Cover and simmer gently for 20 to 30 minutes. Meanwhile, mix onions, garlic, and rice. Heat olive oil in large, heavy skillet; add rice mixture. Stir until oil is well mixed in. Cover and fry very gently for 10 minutes. Stir often and take care mixture does not brown. Add remaining salt, paprika, pepper, parsley, bay leaf, and saffron to chicken pot. Add any of the optional seasonings. Taste to adjust seasonings to your liking. Spread rice mixture over top of chicken. Cover and simmer gently until rice is soft and chicken is tender, 40 to 60 minutes. Add the pimientos just before serving.

Time: 1 hour and 10 to 40 minutes
Servings: 6

This recipe can easily be doubled. It can also be made ahead of time. In fact, it improves with standing as the flavors are absorbed by the rice.

Glazed Strawberry Pie

1 qt. ripe strawberries	1 T. lemon juice
1 (8- or 9-inch) pie shell, baked	1/4 tsp. salt
1 c. sugar	1/2 pt. heavy cream, whipped, or 1 c. frozen whipped topping, thawed
3 T. cornstarch	
1/2 c. water	

Cut half of berries in half, reserving 6 berries with stems left on for garnish. Put the halved berries in pie shell. Crush remaining berries and combine with sugar, cornstarch, water, lemon juice, and salt. Cook gently until thick and clear; cool. Pour cooked mixture over berries in pie shell. Chill. Put ring of whipped cream around top of pie and decorate with reserved berries.

Servings: 6 or 8

𝔘𝔫𝔦𝔱𝔢𝔡 𝔖𝔱𝔞𝔱𝔢𝔰 𝔖𝔢𝔫𝔞𝔱𝔢

WASHINGTON, D. C.

A New Mexico Lunch with a Senator in Washington, D.C.

* Cheese Straws
* Tapas
* El Tamarindo Corn Soup
* Tarragon Chicken Breasts with Asparagus
* Poached Pears with Raspberry Vinegar

Anne Bingaman and the
Honorable Jeff Bingaman   *Washington, D.C.*

The Honorable Jeff Bingaman is a member of the United States Senate from New Mexico. His wife, Anne, has been appointed by President Clinton to head the Antitrust Division of the Department of Justice.

Cheese Straws

1 pkg. frozen puff pastry
1/2 c. grated Parmesan cheese
2 to 3 dashes ground Hatch
   red chile, of course!

1/2 tsp. salt
1/4 tsp. freshly ground black
   pepper

In a small bowl, mix together all ingredients but the puff pastry. Roll out the pastry into a 7x12-inch rectangle. Press the cheese mixture into both sides of the pastry. Cut pastry into 1/2-inch wide ribbons. Using both hands, grasp the ends of each ribbon and twist in opposite directions to create a rippled effect. Place on a greased cookie sheet. Bake at 400° until straws are puffed and lightly browned, about 12 minutes. Store in an airtight container.

Time: 12 minutes
Temperature: 400°
Yield: 24 straws

Serve with soup.

Tapas

4 oz. best quality black olives
4 oz. green cured olives
1 lb. small, spiced shrimp, cooked, peeled & chilled (may be purchased already prepared)
1 can smoked oysters, drained
1 can skinless & boneless sardines, drained
1 can anchovies, drained
1 c. shelled & salted nuts, such as almonds, filberts or pecans
1 jar hot pickled okra
Pepperoni slices
12 slices prosciutto, wrapped around 12 melon wedges
Deviled eggs
1 (9 oz.) jar pickled vegetables (Italian giardinera), drained
Syrian string cheese
8 oz. bleu cheese, cut into bite-size cubes or wedges
1 jar marinated artichoke hearts, drained

If you are looking for something simple, but different, consider starting the meal with Spanish-type appetizers and a glass of dry sherry. Choose 4 to 6 items from the list above. Arrange in small bowls or plates on a tray. Provide your guests with plates and forks and let them select their favorites. For you, serving will be a matter of wielding a can opener.

Servings: 6

El Tamarindo Corn Soup

4 c. fresh or thawed, frozen corn
1 (4 oz.) can chopped green chiles (fresh is best)
2 garlic cloves, minced
1 tsp. oregano
1 tsp. cumin
2 1/2 c. chicken broth, divided
1 1/2 c. milk
Salt & freshly-ground pepper to taste
1 c. peeled, diced tomato (for garnish)
1/2 c. chopped green onions (for garnish)
1/2 c. chopped cilantro or parsley (for garnish)

Add corn, chiles, garlic, oregano, cumin, and 1 cup chicken broth to processor or blender and purée. Transfer to a saucepan and add remaining broth, milk, and salt and pepper. Bring to a gentle boil; reduce heat and simmer about 10 minutes, stirring occasionally. Transfer to a container and refrigerate several hours or several days.

Ladle soup into terra cotta bowls, if available, and garnish with tomatoes, green onions and cilantro. Servings: 6

This soup is a wonderful combination of textures and shapes: smooth and crunchy, cold and hot. Great with Cheese Straws.

Tarragon Chicken Breasts with Asparagus

6 chicken breast halves, boned
  (with skin left on)
24 stalks asparagus, washed
  & trimmed
1 stick butter, at room
  temperature

2 T. dried tarragon, or 4 T.
  minced, fresh tarragon
Salt & freshly-ground black
  pepper to taste
Parsley sprigs & lemon
  rounds for garnish

Lightly flatten chicken breasts. Blend butter and tarragon in small bowl. Divide mixture into 6 portions and spread on interior of each breast. Sprinkle with salt and pepper to taste. Place 4 asparagus stalks in each chicken breast; fold breast over and secure with a toothpick. Spread any leftover butter on top skin of chicken. Place breasts in well-oiled baking dish. Cover with plastic wrap and refrigerate until 1 hour before serving.

To cook chicken, place in preheated 375° oven and bake, uncovered, for about 45 minutes, or until kitchen fork inserts easily and chicken in nicely browned. (Remove toothpicks or warn your guests!)

BLENDER HOLLANDAISE SAUCE:

3 egg yolks
Juice of 1 lemon
Dash of cayenne pepper

1 tsp. salt
1 1/2 sticks butter, melted

Place egg yolks, lemon juice, cayenne pepper, and salt in blender or food processor and blend briefly. With blender running, slowly pour hot butter into egg mixture until well blended. Place in serving container. Cover with plastic wrap and keep at room temperature until serving time. May be made up to 3 hours in advance of serving.

To serve: Place chicken on warm platter and garnish with parsley and lemon. Add a few raspberries to the garnish for color and texture. Pass the hollandaise sauce separately.

Time: 45 minutes
Temperature: 375°
Servings: 6

Poached Pears with Raspberry Vinegar

6 pears, ripe but firm   4 T. raspberry vinegar
3 c. water   3 whole cloves
1 c. sugar

Combine water and sugar in deep saucepan; cook until sugar dissolves. Add vinegar and cloves. Simmer for 10 minutes. Peel pears, leaving on stem; add to syrup. Simmer about 20 minutes, turning several times. Do not overcook.

Transfer pears and syrup to an attractive serving dish; cool. Cover with plastic wrap and refrigerate up to 3 days before serving. Serve pears cold with a little syrup. Add mint leaf to stem as "pear leaf"

Servings: 6

❖

Raspberries and Fiber
Fiber is available in many foods. It aids digestion, may protect against cancer, lowers your cholesterol level, and because it is so filling, reduces the temptation to snack between meals. The most fiber-rich fruits include: FRESH RASPBERRIES, dried or canned prunes, apples, and fresh blackberries.

Saavedra Soup Supper

* Bread Sticks
* Light Vegetable Soup
* Minestrone
  Raspberry Soup (see index)
* Green Chile Stew
* Gypsy Raspberry Brownies (see index)

Gail Saavedra accompanied her menu with the following comments: "We like casual, do-ahead meals that guests often serve themselves. An assortment of fruits, cheeses and crackers provide a nice start while finishing touches are put on soups and bread sticks. In addition to the crackers and bread sticks, I always serve tortillas. I serve Green Chile Stew and Raspberry Soup anytime, but I'm apt to serve the Light Vegetable Soup in warm months, and the Minestrone in the cooler months."

Gail Saavedra   *Albuquerque*

Gail Saavedra is a school counselor in Albuquerque, New Mexico. Her husband, Louis, is a former Mayor of Albuquerque. They have been active supporters of the Very Special Raspberry Festival and Gail is a past chairman of the Raspberry Festival.

Bread Sticks

3 to 3 1/2 c. regular
   all-purpose flour, unsifted
1 T. sugar
1 tsp. salt
1 pkg. active dry yeast

1/2 c. olive or salad oil
1 1/4.c. hot water (120° to
   130°)
1 egg white, beaten with 1 T.
   water
Coarse salt, toasted sesame
   seed or poppy seed (optional)

In large bowl of electric mixer, stir 1 cup flour, sugar, salt, and yeast to blend; add oil. Gradually add hot water and beat at medium speed for 2 minutes. Add 1/2 cup more flour and beat 2 more minutes. Stir or beat in 1 1/2 to 2 cups remaining flour to make a soft dough.

Continued on following page.

Continued from preceding page.

Turn dough onto well-floured board, and with well-floured hands, work into a smooth ball. Shape into an even log and cut into equal-sized pieces according to preference. Roll into rope of desired length and place on oiled baking sheets or on foil-covered oven racks which have been oiled. Roll to grease all sides of dough.

Set in a warm place, covered, and let rise until puffy, about 15 minutes. Brush each stick with egg white and water; sprinkle with salt or seeds, or leave plain. Bake at 325° for 20 to 25 minutes, until lightly browned all over.

Though this dough can be shaped and frozen unbaked, then thawed and baked as above, it is preferable to bake and then freeze. Sticks can be thawed and oven-crisped just before serving.

Time: 20 to 25 minutes
Temperature: 325°
Yield: 32 (12-inch) sticks, or 16 to 20 longer sticks

Green Chile Stew

1 lb. (more or less) lean	2 to 3 c. cooked pinto beans
ground beef	1 env. onion soup mix
5 to 6 c. water	2 c. chopped green chile
2 to 3 cooked, cubed potatoes	

Brown ground beef in a 4 1/2-quart soup kettle; drain off excess fat. Add water, potatoes, beans, soup mix, and chile. Simmer until flavors blend.

Use the water in which the potatoes cooked and the bean juice to provide part of the liquid. Raw potatoes can be sliced into the rest of the ingredients and cooked in the stew.

Servings: 6 to 8

This is definitely one of those recipes that is modifiable according to a family's taste. You may want more or less chile, or may add other seasonings. This could be called a "starter stew".

Light Vegetable Soup

2 lg. potatoes, scrubbed
2 c. water
1 c. fresh or frozen peas
1 c. fresh or frozen corn
3 T. butter or margarine
1 c. diced onion
1 1/2 tsp. salt
2 med. carrots

1 c. diced broccoli
1 diced green pepper
2 small (5 to 6 inches) diced
    zucchini
1 qt. milk, warmed
1/2 tsp. thyme, other fresh
    herbs to taste
1/4 tsp. nutmeg

Cook scrubbed potatoes in water until soft. Pour potatoes and water into blender and purée. Put into a 4 1/2-quart soup kettle; add peas and corn.

In heavy skillet, melt butter and cook onion with salt for about 8 minutes. Add other vegetables in order, sautéing about 8 minutes as each is added. When all vegetables are tender, add to potato mixture. Gradually add warm milk to soup. Add seasonings (fresh herb snippets such as thyme, basil or marjoram are an option) to taste. Slowly warm soup through (do not cook, just heat) and serve immediately.

Servings: 6 to 8

Minestrone Soup

3 T. olive oil
1/2 to 3/4 c. chopped onion
4 cloves crushed garlic
2 tsp. salt
1 c. cubed carrots
1 tsp. oregano
1/2 tsp. black pepper
1 tsp. basil
1 c. chopped green pepper
1 c. cubed zucchini
3 1/2 c. water or stock

2 c. tomato purée
1 1/2 c. cooked garbanzo beans
    (3/4 c. raw; if you start
    with raw garbanzos, save
    the cooking water to use as
    part of the stock for fuller
    flavor & higher protein)
3 T. dry red wine
1 c. fresh, chopped tomatoes
1/2 c. dry pasta
Grated Parmesan cheese

Using a 4 1/2-quart soup kettle, sauté onion and garlic in oil until soft and translucent. Add 1 teaspoon salt and the carrot; mix well. Add oregano, black pepper and basil. Cover and cook over low heat 5 to 10 minutes. Add pepper, zucchini, stock, purée, cooked beans and wine. Cover and simmer 15 minutes. Add tomatoes and remaining teaspoon salt. Keep at lowest heat until 10 minutes before serving. Heat to a boil; add pasta and boil gently until pasta is tender. Serve immediately, topped with Parmesan cheese.

Servings: 6 to 8

The University of New Mexico

Sunday Brunch at University House

* Raspberry Punch
* Caviar Egg Mold with assorted crackers
* Raspberry and Spinach Salad
* Torta Primavera
  Fresh Tomatoes with Fresh Basil Vinaigrette
  Assorted Finger Desserts
     Chocolate Caramel Squares
     Lemon Squares
     * Pizzelles

Donna Peck and Dr. Richard Peck   *Albuquerque*

University House is the home of Richard and Donna Peck. Dr. Peck is President of the University of New Mexico. The house is located on the campus in Albuquerque. The house was built in 1930 in Spanish Pueblo Revival Style and is on the National Register of Historic Buildings. The Pecks entertain at the house often. This is a brunch menu they have used.

Raspberry Punch

2 (10 oz.) pkg. frozen red
   raspberries in syrup, thawed
1/3 c. lemon juice concentrate
1/2 c. sugar

1 (750 ml.) New Mexican rosé
   wine, chilled
1 qt. raspberry sherbet
1 (750 ml.) btl. New Mexican
   champagne, chilled

Purée raspberries in blender. Combine raspberries, lemon concentrate, sugar and wine. Stir until sugar dissolves. Just before serving, scoop sherbet into punch and add champagne. Stir gently.

Yield: 2 quarts

Caviar Egg Mold

2 green onions, tops included	1 T. unflavored gelatin
3 oz. cream cheese	2 T. hot water
6 eggs, hard-cooked	1/2 c. Spanish onions,
1/2 c. mayonnaise	chopped
2 tsp. lemon juice	1 c. sour cream
1/2 tsp. salt	3 1/2 oz. canned red or black
	caviar

In food processor or blender, place green onion (cut in fourths) and cream cheese. Blend until onion is chopped. Add eggs, mayonnaise, lemon juice, and salt. Blend again until eggs are smooth. Dissolve gelatin in hot water. Stir it well and allow it to stand 5 minutes. Add to mixture in blender. Blend 2 seconds. Pour into mixing bowl and stir in Spanish onions. Pour mixture into an oiled 2-cup mold and refrigerate overnight, until set.

Right before serving, unmold and spread sour cream over mold. Spoon and spread caviar over top of sour cream. Serve with a thinly sliced, toasted baguette or Melba rounds. Garnish with slices or wedges of hard-cooked eggs and parsley.

Servings: 8 to 10

Raspberry Spinach Salad

SALAD:

7 c. spinach, rinsed, stemmed	2 kiwis, peeled & sliced
& torn into pieces	5 radishes, sliced
1/2 c. nuts (piñon or	4 scallions, sliced (opt.)
macadamia nuts are good)	
1 c. fresh raspberries	

Toss spinach with radishes, scallions, 1/2 the nuts, 1/2 the raspberries, and 1/2 the kiwis with the dressing in a bowl. Top with remaining nuts, raspberries and kiwis. Serve immediately.

DRESSING:

2 T. red wine vinegar	1 1/3 c. vegetable oil
2 T. raspberry jam	1 T. minced onion

Combine vinegar and jam in blender or small bowl. Add oil in a very thin stream, blending well. Add onions.

Servings: 8

Torta Primavera

CRUST:
1 lb. puff pastry (homemade
   or purchased)

Roll out 3/4 of the pastry 1/4-inch thick. Line the bottom and sides of a lightly greased 9-inch springform pan with it. Keep remaining pastry refrigerated.

SPINACH MIXTURE:

1 T. oil	2 T. dried basil
1 T. butter	2 garlic cloves, minced
2 lb. fresh spinach, blanched	2 T. Parmesan cheese
& drained	Salt & pepper

Heat oil and butter in a large skillet. Add spinach, basil and garlic. Sauté for 2 to 3 minutes. Season with salt and pepper and Parmesan cheese. Remove from skillet.

RED PEPPER:

3 lg. red peppers, cut into	1/2 T. olive oil
thick strips	

Add peppers to skillet with oil. Sauté for 2 minutes. Remove from heat and set aside.

OPEN-FACE OMELETS:

Butter, margarine or nonfat	1 tsp. chopped chives
cooking spray	1 T. chopped parsley
3 eggs, beaten	Salt & pepper
1 T. half & half	

Grease bottom of an 8-inch omelet pan. Combine ingredients and divide in half. Use each half to make an omelet for a total of 2 omelets.

TO ASSEMBLE THE TORTA:
1 lb. Swiss cheese, thinly sliced
1 lb. baked ham, thinly sliced
1 egg, beaten

Position rack in lower third of oven and preheat to 350°.

Continued on following page.

Continued from preceding page.

Layer ingredients in prepared pan in the following order:

1 omelet	1/2 of the ham
1/2 of the spinach mixture	All the red pepper
1/2 of the cheese	

Repeat in reverse order: balance of ham, cheese, spinach mixture, and ending with the remaining omelet.

Roll remaining pastry 1/4-inch thick and cut out a 9 1/2-inch circle. Place over omelet and seal it well into pastry lining by pinching with fingers. With top of knife, draw the number of slices desired directly on pastry or decorate with scoops of pastry. Brush with beaten egg.

Place pan on baking sheet and bake at 375° until golden brown, 70 to 75 minutes. Cool slightly. Release from pan and serve warm or at room temperature.

Time: 70 to 75 minutes
Temperature: 375°
Servings: 10 to 12

Pizzelle

(An Italian Wafer Cookie)

3 eggs	1/2 tsp. anise seeds
3/4 c. sugar	1/2 tsp. anise extract
1/2 c. butter or margarine,	1 3/4 c. flour
melted & cooled	2 tsp. baking powder
1/2 tsp. vanilla extract	

Beat eggs and sugar. Add butter or margarine, vanilla and anise. (Put the anise seeds in a small plastic bag and use a rolling pin to crush them. This makes them more flavorful.) Sift flour and baking powder; add to egg mixture. Batter will be stiff enough to be dropped by spoon.

Heat and use pizzelle iron according to directions on the package. (A pizzelle iron is available at most gourmet cooking stores.)

Yield: 3 to 4 dozen

The cookies can be stored in an airtight container for at least 1 month.

Entertaining the Anderson School Supporters

* Cheese English Muffins
* Roasted Pepper and Garbanzo Salad
  French Bread
* Baked Chicken Kiev
* Green Chile Rice
* Raspberry Cream Angel Food Cake

Karla and Ken Walters   *Seattle, WA*

Ken is a former Dean of the Anderson School of Business at the University of New Mexico. Karla entertained the business community frequently, especially before sporting or fine arts events. She has received "Bravos" for her excellent culinary skills when she serves this menu.

Cheese English Muffins

6 English muffins, split
1/2 to 3/4 lb. Cheddar
   cheese, grated
1 lg. onion, chopped fine

1 sm. can chopped olives
1/4 tsp. curry powder
2 T. mayonnaise, or enough
   to bind

Combine all ingredients with just enough mayonnaise to hold mixture together. Spread on halved English muffins. Cut the muffins into quarters to make small, bite-size pieces. Bake on cookie sheets at 350° until cheese melts, 5 to 7 minutes. Serve hot.

Servings: 8 to 12

Roasted Pepper and Garbanzo Salad

PEPPERS:
6 red or green bell peppers

Set whole peppers in a shallow pan and place under preheated broiler, about 1-inch from heat source. Broil. Turn frequently with tongs, until peppers are well-blistered and charred on all sides. Place in a paper bag. Close the bag tightly and let peppers sweat for 20 minutes to loosen skins. Cool and strip off skins under cold running water. Cut peppers in half and remove; discard stems and seeds. Cut peppers into thin strips.

DRESSING:

1 clove garlic, minced	1/2 tsp. salt
1/3 c. olive oil	1/4 tsp. pepper
2 T. balsamic vinegar	1/2 c. cooked garbanzo beans

In a medium bowl, whisk together garlic, olive oil, vinegar, salt and pepper. Add the peppers and garbanzo beans to the dressing. Toss lightly and refrigerate at least 2 hours, or for a day.

TO ASSEMBLE:
3 lg. tomatoes, peeled
20 pitted, ripe olives
1 head bibb lettuce

Immediately before serving, cut the tomatoes into wedges and add to the peppers along with the olives. Drain, reserving liquid. Line a serving platter or large, shallow bowl with lettuce. Arrange pepper mixture on lettuce and drizzle reserved dressing over top. Accompany with crusty French bread.

Servings: 8

Baked Chicken Kiev

4 whole chicken breasts,	1/2 tsp. garlic salt
skinned, boned & split	1/4 tsp. pepper
1/2 c. fine, dry bread crumbs	1/4 c. butter, softened
1/2 c. grated Parmesan cheese	1 T. chopped parsley
1 1/2 tsp. oregano leaves	6 T. melted butter

Place chicken, one piece at a time, skinned-side down, between 2 pieces of plastic wrap and pound with a flat-surfaced mallet until about 1/8-inch thick. In a shallow bowl, combine bread crumbs, Parmesan cheese, 1 teaspoon of the oregano, garlic salt and pepper; set aside. In a small bowl, stir together butter, remaining 1/2 teaspoon oregano and parsley.

Arrange pounded chicken pieces, skinned-side down. Spread about 1/2 tablespoon of the butter mixture across each piece about an inch from one long side; fold short ends over filling, then fold in long side and roll to enclose filling. Dip each bundle in the melted butter and drain briefly. Roll it in crumb mixture until evenly coated.

Place bundles, seam-side down and slightly separated, in a 10x15-inch rimmed baking pan that has been lined with foil. Drizzle with any remaining butter. Cover and refrigerate for at least 4 hours, or until the next day. Bake, uncovered, at 425° until chicken is no longer pink when lightly slashed, about 20 minutes. Serve immediately.

Time: 20 minutes
Temperature: 425°
Servings: 8

Green Chile Rice

1 c. rice, cooked (to make 3 c.)
1/4 c. butter, melted
1 pt. sour cream
1/8 c. milk
1/2 lb. Monterey Jack cheese,

1 sm. can green chiles
  (or 5 whole roasted,
  peeled chiles)
Salt to taste
Paprika

Mix rice, sour cream, milk and butter. Remove seeds and veins from chiles and dice them. Alternate layers of rice mixture, cheese and chiles in a 1 1/2- or 2-quart casserole. Sprinkle paprika lightly on top. Bake at 350° until mixture bubbles, approximately 30 minutes.

Time: 30 minutes
Temperature: 350°
Servings: 8
(Doubled recipe fills a 9x13-inch casserole and serves up to 20 as a side dish.)

This tastes excellent the next day.

Raspberry Cream
Angel Food Cake

1 pt. heavy cream
2 T. confectioners' sugar

3 pt. fresh raspberries,
  sugared to taste (or 3 pkg.
  frozen raspberries)
1 lg. angel food cake

Chill cream, mixing bowl and beater. Whip cream until stiff, adding confectioners' sugar as cream begins to stiffen. If whipped ahead of time, cover tightly and chill.

Just before serving, stir the cream and fold in raspberries. Slice angel food cake into wedges. Top each slice with a generous serving of raspberry cream.

Servings: 8

Tailgating at UNM's Football Games

* Barbecued Meatballs
* German Potato Salad
  Hard Rolls
* Raspberry Sandwich Cookies
* Raspberry Kir

Kim and Dennis Franchione   *Albuquerque*

Kim Franchione is the wife of the University of New Mexico's football coach, Dennis, or "Coach Fran" as his fans call him. He started his career at UNM in 1992 and made "Frantastic" progress with the "Lobo" football team he inherited. Kim suggests this menu for a tailgate picnic before the football games.

Barbecued Meatballs

MEATBALLS:

1 (13 oz.) can evaporated milk	1/2 tsp. garlic powder
3 lb. ground chuck	1/2 tsp. pepper
2 c. oatmeal	2 tsp. salt
2 eggs	1/2 tsp. chili powder
1 c. chopped onion	

Mix ingredients together and shape into balls the size of walnuts. Place in flat, shallow pan, 1 layer deep.

SAUCE FOR MEATBALLS:

2 c. catsup	1/2 tsp. garlic powder
1 1/2 c. brown sugar	1/2 c. chopped onions
2 T. liquid smoke	

Combine ingredients for sauce. Pour over meatballs and bake at 350° for 1 hour. May be kept warm in a crock-pot.

Time: 1 hour
Temperature: 350°
Servings: 12

German Potato Salad

1/2 c. vegetable oil
1/4 c. vinegar
1/2 tsp. pepper
1 tsp. salt

1 tsp. garlic powder
6 boiled potatoes, peeled
  & cubed

Mix together oil, vinegar, pepper, salt and garlic powder. Pour over cubed potatoes.

Servings: 8

This may be served immediately at room temperature. It is really delicious if refrigerated a couple of hours before serving. Shredded cabbage may be used instead of potatoes.

Raspberry Kir

2 2/3 c. chablis, chilled

1 T. Chambord or other
  raspberry liqueur

Pour 2/3 cup wine in each wine glass. Add 3/4 teaspoon Chambord to each one; stir well.

Servings: 4

This can be mixed in larger quantities just before being served, and reserved in a Thermos-type container.

Raspberry Sandwich Cookies

1 c. butter, softened
2/3 c. sugar
2 egg yolks
1 1/2 c. all-purpose flour
1/4 tsp. salt
1 to 2 T. confectioners' sugar
1/2 c. sugar

1/2 c. ground, blanched
   almonds
2 egg whites
1 1/2 c. raspberry preserves
   (approximately)
Confectioners' sugar (optional)
1/2 c. semisweet chocolate
   morsels, melted

Cream butter. Gradually add sugar, beating at medium speed until light and fluffy. Add egg yolks, one at a time, beating well. Combine flour and salt; add to creamed mixture, beating well. Shape dough into a ball. Cover or wrap and chill at least 2 hours.

Using half of the dough at a time, roll to 1/8-inch thickness and cut one half of it with 2 1/2-inch doughnut cutter, reserving centers. Cut the other half using a 2 1/2-inch round cutter. (Chill dough again if necessary.)

Combine 1/2 cup sugar and almonds; mix well. Beat egg whites until frothy. Brush one side of cookie cut-outs with egg white and coat with almond mixture. Place coated side up on lightly greased cookie sheets. Repeat procedure with remaining dough. Bake at 375° for 8 to 10 minutes. Cool on wire racks.

Spread uncoated side of each solid cookie with a thin layer of raspberry preserves. Lightly dust almond side of doughnut-shaped cookies with confectioners' sugar, if desired. Place sugar-side up on top of raspberry filling. Frost with melted chocolate morsels.

Time: 8 to 10 minutes
Temperature: 375°
Yield: 2 dozen

❖

Using Raspberries
Berries deteriorate quickly, but raspberries suffer the most because they may mold within 24 hours of picking. This makes them scarce and expensive, but red raspberries remain a favorite, whatever their price. Be sure to use them in recipes where their flavor is not overwhelmed by other strong ingredients.

A Special Meal at Dixon's Apple Orchard

* Stuffed Jalapeños
* Garden Twirls Pasta Salad
  Sliced Baked Ham and Cheeses
  Freshly Baked Rolls
* Apple Pie with
* Foolproof Pie Crust

Dixon's Apples   *Peña Blanca*

Dixon's Apple Orchard is located a few miles off Interstate 25 in the small town of Peña Blanca, New Mexico. The orchards are managed by Becky Dixon-Mullane and her grandfather, Fred Dixon. This menu was served at the Dixon-Mullane wedding when Becky married Jim during apple blossom time in 1993. Becky catered the meal herself and it received rave reviews.

Stuffed Jalapeños

1 (2 oz.) can jalapeño peppers   1 (4 1/4 oz.) can deviled ham,
                                        roast beef, or chicken

Cut stems off jalapeños and cut in half. Cut membrane out from center of jalapeño halves. Wash jalapeños thoroughly. Stuff halves with meat. Arrange on relish plate.

Servings: 6 to 10

Your choice of meat to use for stuffing depends on the rest of the menu. Whatever your choice, this is always a favorite among guests.

Garden Twirls Pasta Salad

1 (12 oz.) pkg. tomato &
  spinach garden twirls pasta
1 (8 oz.) can sliced water
  chestnuts
1/4 c. pitted black olives
1/4 c. pitted green olives
1/2 c. cauliflower flowerets

1/2 c. broccoli flowerets
1/2 c. diagonally-sliced celery
1 c. frozen peas, partially
  thawed
1 pkg. Italian salad dressing
  mix
Oil & vinegar

Prepare macaroni according to directions on package; rinse with cool water. Drain water chestnuts. Slice olives, draining well. Combine all ingredients, except for dressing. Mix salad dressing according to directions on package. Pour on salad and toss.

Servings: 8 to 10

Salad may be refrigerated for a few hours before serving, which makes the flavors blend even better. This salad is great for picnics.

Foolproof Pie Crust

4 c. flour
1 3/4 c. solid vegetable
  shortening
1 T. sugar

2 tsp. salt
1 T. vinegar
1 egg, beaten
1/2 c. water

With a fork, mix together flour, shortening, sugar and salt. In a separate bowl, beat together vinegar, egg and water. Combine mixtures and, stirring with a fork, mold into a ball. Chill at least 15 minutes.

Dough can be left in the refrigerator up to 3 days, or it can be frozen. Use lots of flour when rolling out.

Yield: 2 double pie crusts

Becky's comment:
"This is truly the best crust I have ever made or eaten. It was given to me by Mrs. Strebe, who was a minister's wife. I have thanked and blessed her many times for passing this recipe on to me."

Dixon's Apple Pie

8 Champagne apples	2 T. butter
1/2 c. sugar	Foolproof pastry for 2-crust
1 1/2 T. flour	pie

Preheat oven to 400°. Peel and cut apples very fine. Put in a sealable plastic bag with the sugar and flour. Seal bag shut and shake well. Put coated apples in pie shell and dot with butter. Roll out the other crust and place on top of apples. Sprinkle crust with white sugar. Bake at 400° for 10 minutes. Reduce heat and bake at 350° until apples are done.

Time and temperature: 10 minutes at 400°, 25 to 30 minutes at 350°
Servings: 6 to 8

The Dixons prefer the flavor of the apples, so they do not add cinnamon.

Champagne apples are unique to New Mexico. The fruit was hybridized by Fred Dixon. Although he has had requests from other orchards in different parts of the country, he has not sold any of the trees.

❖

A Savory Morning Treat; Fruit Spread on Waffle or Pancakes
Transform waffles and pancakes into savory morning treats. Top them with a fabulous fruit spread. Place lowfat vanilla yogurt in a strainer and drain over bowl overnight in the refrigerator. Combine "cheese" portion remaining in strainer with raspberries. Add a dash of flavor with cinnamon, ginger or nutmeg.

Maggie's Breakfast Menu

* Maggie's Oatmeal
* Yogurt and Apricot Créme
  Fresh Rhubarb and Strawberries
  Raspberry Spread (see index)
  Baked Bread with Jams
* Baked Egg Dish
  Coffee and Tea
  Fresh Juices

Maggie Lilley   *Albuquerque*

Maggie Lilley is the owner of Maggie's Raspberry Ranch, a Bed and Breakfast in Albuquerque's North Valley. Maggie is noted for her outstanding breakfasts using raspberries she grows on her property. She picks them fresh for her guests each morning. She shares raspberry tips and other recipes throughout the book.

Maggie's Oatmeal

1/3 c. brown sugar	1/2 tsp. margarine
1 tsp. salt	1 c. oatmeal
3 c. water	1 c. sweetened applesauce

In a medium-sized saucepan, combine sugar, salt, water and margarine. Add oatmeal and boil gently for 10 minutes. Add applesauce. Bring back to a boil. Cover and remove from heat. Let stand at least 5 minutes before serving. Do not stir more than necessary because too much stirring causes sticky oatmeal.

Servings: 6 to 8

Yogurt and Apricot Créme

1 (32 oz.) ctn. plain yogurt   Puréed apricots
2 heaping T. confectioners'
  sugar

Add sugar to yogurt and stir well. Using a 6-inch tall x 4-inch wide glass, layer equal amounts of yogurt mixture and apricots, ending with apricots. Top with a sprig of mint and a few fresh raspberries.

Servings: 6 to 8

Baked Egg Dish

Day-old bread   Cream cheese, softened
Eggs, beaten   & sweetened
Sugar   Raspberry jelly
Plain yogurt or milk

Break bread into pieces. Cover with beaten eggs, sugar and yogurt. Refrigerate overnight. In the morning, pour into a lightly-oiled baking dish. Press bread into dish to make smooth on top. Cover and bake at 350° for 30 minutes. Remove from oven. Add sweetened cream cheese. Top with a thin layer of raspberry jelly. Slice and serve hot.

Time: 30 minutes
Temperature: 350°
Servings: 1 per egg

Maggie does not have a specific recipe for this dish. She uses an egg for each guest. She adds the other ingredients for consistency and taste. She says it is always a great success.

❖

Maggie on Growing Raspberries
Flower clusters must be pollinated, so big fat bees are vital to big, fat berries. If you don't see lots of honey bees working the flowers, don't wait for nature to take its course - get a hive.

30

Historic Farm Dinner

Corn, Tomato and Summer Squash Soup
Mixed Green Salad with Peppery Sharp Arugula, Tangy
   Red Mustard and Spicy Curly Cress
* Southwestern-Style Chicken Salad with Cilantro
Roasted Assorted Peppers with Fresh Herbs
Hearty Breads
* Swedish Cream with Berries
* Mexican Chocolate Cookies
Wine from the New Mexican Vineyard across the street

Penny Rembe and Dr. Armin Rembe   *Albuquerque*

Five miles from the center of Albuquerque, a new organic farm is growing on the old historic Los Poblanos Ranch. Los Poblanos was originally a grant from the Spanish Crown extending from the tops of the Sandia mountains to the Rio Grande river. The ranch was restored by John Gaw Meem in 1932 for Albert and Ruth Hanna McCormick Simms. They turned Los Poblanos into an experimental farm, creating the most modern dairy in the industry at that time. The Rembes bought the property from the Simms family in 1977. They have restored the flower gardens, raise churro sheep, and are venturing into the organic vegetable business. Many of the vegetables they grow are from native seeds, emphasizing historical background with flavor and simple preparation. This country supper for neighbors is typical.

Southwestern Chicken Salad

DRESSING:

1/4 c. vegetable oil	1/2 tsp. salt
1/4 c. olive oil	1/2 tsp. sugar
1/4 c. lime juice	1 T. chili powder
1 tsp. ground cumin	2 cloves garlic

In small bowl, stir together oil, lime juice, cumin, salt, sugar, chili powder and garlic.

SALAD:

3 c. cooked chicken, julienned	1/4 c. red onion, chopped
1 (7 oz.) can kernel corn, drained (2 to 3 ears fresh corn from the garden is better, boiled & cut off cob)	1 (4 oz.) can chopped green chile, drained
	1/4 c. cilantro, chopped
1 c. red pepper, julienned	Assorted lettuce leaves

In large bowl, mix chicken, corn, red pepper, red onion, chiles and cilantro. Add dressing and toss to coat well. Cover. Refrigerate at least 2 hours. Serve on lettuce-lined serving platter.

Servings: 6

Swedish Cream with Berries

1 pkg. gelatin	1 tsp. vanilla
1 pt. heavy cream	2 or 3 pkg. frozen raspberries
1 c. sugar	(or 2 of raspberries & 1 of
1 pt. sour cream	boysenberries)

Sprinkle gelatin on a quarter cup of heavy cream until it is completely softened. Mix with the rest of the cream and sugar over low heat. Stir gently until gelatin is completely dissolved. Cool until slightly thickened. Fold in sour cream and vanilla. (Do not beat, just fold.)

Pour into soufflé dish or pretty bowl and chill until set. Drain berries and cover cream; serve.

Servings: 4 to 6

Mexican Chocolate Cookies

COOKIES:

1 c. butter or margarine	2 1/2 c. flour
1 1/2 c. confectioners' sugar	2 oz. unsweetened chocolate, melted
1 egg	1 tsp. cinnamon
1 tsp. vanilla	1 tsp. ground black pepper

Mix butter and sugar until thoroughly blended. Add egg and vanilla; mix. Blend in flour; set aside.

Add cinnamon and pepper to the melted chocolate and mix. Add chocolate mixture to other mixture and blend well. Roll out on floured surface. Cut with round end cookie cutter. Bake at 375° for 5 to 7 minutes. While still warm, dip in cinnamon sugar.

CINNAMON SUGAR:

1/4 c. sugar	1 tsp. baking cocoa
1 T. cinnamon	

Mix the above 3 ingredients. Put in flat dish. Put warm cookies face down in sugar for light coating. Store in closed container.

Time: 5 to 7 minutes
Temperature: 375°
Yield: 5 to 6 dozen (depending on size)

❖

Growing Raspberries in New Mexico
Raspberries produced in the fall taste sweeter. Cool weather tends to retard respiration, making sugar accumulate in the berries.

Santa Fe Opera Tailgate Picnic

Small, boiled red potatoes stuffed with sour cream and
    caviar, topped with fresh dill
Chilled Gazpacho with Chopped Green Pepper, Green Onion
    and Zucchini (or)
Cherry Tomatoes stuffed with Chopped Vegetables and Tiny
    Shrimp
* Tampico Salad
* Cornish Game Hens, Stuffed with Herb Rice Dressing with
    Raspberry Dipping Sauce
* Chocolate Raspberry Mousse (see recipe index)
New Mexico Champagne
Thermos of strong coffee (perhaps raspberry gourmet flavor)

Karen and Bob Turner　　　　　　　　　　　　　　　*Albuquerque*

*Many opera fans enjoy elegant twilight picnics in the opera parking lot
before the outdoor performance begins at 9 p.m. It's fun to stroll through
the parking area to see the spreads. You'll see everything from crystal
stemware and china plates, to take-out chicken on paper plates! But, do
please bring your crystal for the champagne. It's much more festive!*

Tampico Salad

4 avocados, peeled & cubed, sprinkled with lime juice	2 c. fresh pineapple chunks 2 c. fresh jicama, cubed Pomegranate seeds

DRESSING:
1/4 c. fresh lime juice	2 tsp. New Mexico honey
2 T. light vegetable oil	

Combine and immediately pour over avocado, pineapple and
jicama. Mix carefully and thoroughly. Place on lettuce leaves in
your traveling bowl; top with pomegranate seeds.

Servings: 8 to 10

Cornish Game Hens with Rice Dressing

2 T. butter	2 c. cooked rice
1/2 c. chopped onion	1 c. dry bread cubes
4 Cornish game hens, rinse	1/2 tsp. poultry seasoning
& pat dry (may use neck/	1/2 tsp. rosemary
giblets in broth, or save for	1/2 c. unsweetened
another dish)	raspberries
	Butter

Sauté onion in butter. Combine with chopped giblets (if used), raspberries, rice, bread cubes, poultry seasoning and rosemary. Carefully stuff hens, then close cavity with small metal skewers or tie with strings to hold shape. Rub hens generously with butter. Roast at 400° for approximately 1 hour. Check for browning and tenderness. Chill if for a picnic. Serve with raspberry sauce.

Time: 1 hour
Temperature: 400°
Servings: 8

Raspberry Dipping Sauce

Nice and messy, so be sure to take sturdy napkins and dampened fingertip towels.

2 T. cornstarch	2 c. orange juice
2 tsp. dry mustard	2 c. unsweetened raspberries
1 T. grated fresh ginger	1 T. fresh lemon juice
3 T. sugar	Salt & pepper to taste
2 c. chicken broth	2 T. Triple Sec liqueur
3 T. slivered orange peel	

Combine dry ingredients in saucepan. Add 1/2 cup broth and mix thoroughly. Place over heat. Gradually add remaining broth and cook until thick, stirring constantly. Add peel and juice. Allow only to gently simmer, not boil. Add salt and pepper; taste for corrections. Add berries (they will fall apart in the hot sauce, but do not worry). At this point you may want to strain the sauce, although I prefer the texture of the raspberry seeds in the sauce. Add Triple Sec after removing from heat. Serve warm or chilled.

Balloon Fiesta Brunch

*Fruit Yogurt Soup
*Mexican Green Chile Strata
*Santa Fe Tortillas with Raspberry Jam
*Raspberry-Pear Cobbler
*Cafe Mexicano

The Junior League   *Albuquerque*

The Balloon Fiesta is one of Albuquerque's favorite annual events. The mass ascensions start early in the mornings and the roads leading to Fiesta Park are packed with cars and buses as early as 5:00 a.m. Over 500 balloons took part in the 1992 ascension. What better way to celebrate this popular, much-photographed event than with a brunch after you return home! The Junior League suggests this excellent menu of recipes taken from their "Simply Simpatico Cookbook".

Fruit Yogurt Soup

2 (8 oz.) ctn. apricot-flavored
  yogurt
1 c. milk
1/2 c. orange juice

2 T. orange liqueur (opt.)
6 thin orange slices
6 sprigs fresh mint

In medium bowl, combine yogurt, milk, orange juice and liqueur. Stir to mix well. Refrigerate until well chilled, at least 1 hour. Serve in sherbet glasses. Float a thin slice of orange and a sprig of mint on each serving.

Servings: 4 to 6

A cool and refreshing first course.

Mexican Green Chile Strata

6 slices firm bread
Butter
2 c. shredded sharp Cheddar
 cheese
2 c. shredded Monterey Jack
 cheese
8 oz. chopped green chiles

6 eggs
2 c. milk
2 tsp. salt
2 tsp. paprika
1 tsp. crumbled oregano
1/4 tsp. pepper
1/2 tsp. garlic powder
1/4 tsp. dry mustard

Trim crusts from bread and spread one side of each with butter. Arrange bread butter-side down in a 9x12-inch baking pan. Sprinkle cheeses evenly over bread. Distribute the chiles evenly over the cheese layer. In a bowl, beat eggs with milk and all seasonings until well blended. Pour egg mixture over cheese. Cover and chill overnight, or at least 4 hours. Bake, uncovered, at 325° for about 50 minutes, or until top is lightly browned. Let stand 10 minutes before serving.

Time: 50 minutes
Temperature: 325°
Servings: 8

Santa Fe Flour Tortillas

5 c. all-purpose flour
4 tsp. baking powder
1 tsp. salt

1/2 c. bacon drippings
2 c. buttermilk

In a bowl, combine flour, baking powder, and salt. Cut in bacon drippings until fine, even crumbs form. Gradually add buttermilk, mixing with fork until soft, non-sticky dough forms. Knead in bowl 3 to 5 minutes. Divide into 12 to 18 equal pieces. Shape each piece into a smooth ball. To shape each tortilla, flatten a ball of dough to a 3- to 4-inch round. On a floured board, roll each to a 7-inch circle about 1/4-inch thick. Grease heavy, large frying pan with bacon drippings and place over a medium heat. Place dough round in pan and cook slowly, until bubbly and brown, about 2 to 3 minutes on each side.

Preheat oven to 250°. After tortillas are cooked, put them directly on the rack in the oven for 5 minutes. Remove and stack 5 or 6 at a time in foil and return to warm oven until serving time. They hold well up to 2 hours. Serve with butter and honey.

Yield: 12 tortillas

Raspberry Pear Cobbler

1 (10 oz.) pkg. frozen
   raspberries, thawed
1/3 c. sugar
2 tsp. cornstarch
1/4 tsp. ground cinnamon
3 med. fresh or canned pears,
   sliced (2 1/2 c.)

1/2 c. sugar
1 c. flour
1 tsp. baking powder
1/4 tsp. salt
1 beaten egg
3/4 c. sour cream
2 T. butter, melted

Drain raspberries, reserving syrup. Add enough water to syrup to make 1 cup. In saucepan, combine sugar, cornstarch and cinnamon. Add syrup. Cook and stir until bubbly. Add fruits; heat through. Pour into a 10x6-inch baking dish. Combine dry ingredients. Combine the egg, sour cream and butter; add to flour mixture. Blend well. Drop by spoon onto fruit. Bake 30 minutes at 350°.

Time: 30 minutes
Temperature: 350°
Servings: 6 to 8

Cafe Mexicano

1 oz. coffee liqueur
1/2 oz. brandy
1 tsp. chocolate syrup

Dash of ground cinnamon
Hot coffee
Sweetened whipped cream

Combine coffee liqueur, brandy, chocolate syrup and cinnamon in a coffee cup or mug. Fill to the top with hot coffee. Top with whipped cream.

Servings: 1

Salman's on Growing Raspberries Commercially
Raspberries require plenty of water and, depending on soil conditions, some
fertilizer, nitrogen in particular. To grow raspberries commercially requires
significant capital investment, management, sales and a great amount of labor,
plus plenty of good luck.

♥A New Mexico Fall Menu

* Tortilla Soup
* Spinach Salad with Raspberries and Piñons
* Chimayo Chicken Paprikash with Fideo
* Raspberry Soufflé with a Duet of Sauces

Dr. Barry Ramo and Mary Gutierrez, R.D.   *Albuquerque*

Submitted by Dr. Barry Ramo of the New Mexico Heart Clinic, Ltd. Dr. Ramo is also featured on the ABC TV affiliate in Albuquerque with his news feature called "Health Beat". These recipes were compiled by Mary Gutierrez, R.D. at Presbyterian Hospital's Heart Institute in Albuquerque.

"It is fall in New Mexico. The sky is full of hot air balloons and the air is redolent of roasting green chiles. This hearty and heart healthy menu delivers some of the delicious flavors of New Mexico with a very low-fat emphasis. For the entire meal, total fat per serving is a mere 4 grams. (Adding piñons to our salad would increase the fat slightly.) Heart Healthy cooking and New Mexico foods—the perfect combination."

Dr. Barry Ramo

♥Tortilla Soup

1 bunch green onions, sliced
    thinly on the diagonal
8 cloves garlic, roasted
8 sm. Roma tomatoes, peeled,
    seeded & chopped
1 c. green chile, roasted, peeled
    & chopped (or use frozen)
3 (14 oz.) cans low-sodium
    chicken broth

4 T. fresh cilantro leaves
1/2 c. Soubise sauce (optional)
8 corn tortillas, cut in thin
    strips & baked at 300° until
    crisp
Garnishes: non-fat sour
    cream, lime wedges,
    chopped jalapeños

Place green onions in a soup pot with tightly-fitting lid. Add a little broth or white wine to steam. Prepare garlic by simmering whole, unpeeled cloves in water for 5 minutes. Drain and peel. Set on a baking sheet in a 300° oven for 20 minutes. While garlic is roasting, prepare tomatoes, measure chile and open broth.

Mash roasted garlic while adding to onions; add tomatoes, chile and broth. Cook 30 minutes. Add cilantro and cook an additional 15 minutes, thickening with Soubise Sauce if desired. Ladle into bowls and float tortilla strips on top. Pass the garnishes.

♥SOUBISE SAUCE:
1 c. diced onion
3 cloves garlic, minced
1/2 c. long-grain rice
1/2 c. non-fat dry milk powder

1 qt. chicken stock
    (homemade, canned or
    reconstituted with bouillon
    granules; low-sodium
    preferred)

Place onion and garlic in a heavy saucepan; cook over low heat, stirring constantly, for about 5 minutes. Add rice, milk powder and stock. Cook for about 45 minutes, until rice is tender. Transfer to food processor or blender; process until smooth. The mixture will keep in the refrigerator several days to be used as a non-fat thickening agent.

Servings: 8

♥Spinach Salad with Raspberries and Roasted Piñons

2 lg. bunches fresh spinach, washed, stemmed & torn into bite-size pieces
1 pt. fresh raspberries
1 bunch green onions, sliced
Roasted piñon nuts (optional) (1 T. has 5 grams fat)

Mix ingredients. Toss with champagne vinaigrette just before serving.

CHAMPAGNE VINAIGRETTE:
1/2 c. pink grapefruit juice
1/2 c. champagne vinegar
1/4 c. cold water
1 sm. clove garlic, finely chopped
1/2 tsp. black pepper, freshly ground
1 tsp. basil, finely chopped
1/2 tsp. fresh parsley, finely chopped
1 tsp. sugar

Mix all ingredients well in a small nonreactive bowl and chill. It will keep well in the refrigerator for several days.

Yield: 1 cup
Servings: 8

♥Chimayo Chicken Paprikash

Cooking spray
1/2 lb. fresh mushrooms, sliced
1 lg. white onion, thinly sliced
4 cloves garlic, finely minced
4 whole chicken breasts, halved, skinned, boned & trimmed of all fat
1 squeeze of lemon or lime (opt.)
2 c. chicken broth
1 to 2 T. Chimayo chile powder (to taste)
1 (16 oz.) ctn. nonfat sour cream
3 T. flour
1 (10 oz.) bag fideo (vermicelli), cooked according to pkg. directions

Spray large nonstick cooking skillet with cooking spray. Sauté mushrooms, onion and garlic until golden. Remove vegetables from pan and spray again lightly. Add chicken breasts and sauté approximately 3 to 5 minutes per side. Dissolve chile powder in broth and add to chicken. Add lime squeeze. Return vegetables to pan and simmer approximately 10 minutes. Mix flour with nonfat sour cream. Just before serving, slowly whisk sour cream mixture into chicken and warm through. Serve over drained fideo. (Can also be served over rice.) Garnish the plate with a sprig of basil leaves.

Servings: 8

♥Raspberry Soufflé

1 1/3 c. fresh or unsweetened frozen raspberries	2 T. Chambord (raspberry liqueur)
5 T. sugar	5 lg. egg whites
1 1/2 tsp. grated orange zest	1/4 tsp. cream of tartar
2 T. cornstarch	Pinch of salt
1 1/2 T. fresh lemon juice	Confectioners' sugar for dusting top of soufflé

Combine raspberries, sugar and grated orange zest in small saucepan and bring to a boil over medium heat, mashing raspberries. Dissolve cornstarch in lemon juice and add to raspberry mixture. Cook, stirring for about 1 minute, or until thickened and no longer cloudy. Remove from heat and stir in Chambord and remaining raspberries. Transfer to a bowl and allow to come to room temperature. (Mixture can be made in advance. At this point, refrigerate; bring back to room temperature before proceeding.)

Beat egg whites in large bowl until foamy. Add cream of tartar and salt; continue beating until soft peaks form. Gradually add sugar, beating until stiff peaks form. Stir the raspberry mixture and whisk about 1/4 of the beaten egg whites into the raspberry mixture. Fold the resulting raspberry mixture into the remaining egg whites.

Spray the inside of a 1 1/2-quart soufflé dish with non-stick spray and sprinkle with sugar, shaking out excess sugar. Turn the soufflé mixture into the soufflé dish and smooth the top of the soufflé. Place dish in a roasting pan and pour hot water into the pan until the level reaches 1/3 of the way up the dish. Bake for about 35 minutes at 350° with the rack positioned in the lower third of the oven. Dust with confectioners' sugar and serve immediately.

Serve with duet of sauces: Raspberry Sauce and Chocolate Sauce. Place sauces on either side of the plate. With a knife, draw lines across the surface of the plate to mingle the flavors and colors. Place soufflé in the center. Garnish with raspberries and slices of kiwi.

Time: 35 minutes
Temperature: 350°
Servings: 6 to 8

♥Raspberry Sauce

2 c. fresh or unsweetened
   frozen raspberries
2 T. sugar

1 T. cornstarch
3 T. Chambord (raspberry
   liqueur)

In a small saucepan, over medium heat, bring raspberries and sugar to a boil, mashing raspberries. Dissolve cornstarch in 2 tablespoons water and add to the raspberry mixture. Cook, stirring, for 30 to 45 seconds, until thickened or no longer cloudy. Strain through a fine mesh sieve into a bowl. Stir in liqueur and allow sauce to cool. May be made ahead and served chilled, or served at room temperature.

Yield: 1 1/2 cups

♥Chocolate Sauce

1/3 c. unsweetened cocoa
   powder
1 T. cornstarch
1 T. sugar
1/2 c. light or dark corn syrup

1/3 c. skim milk
1 tsp. vegetable oil
1 tsp. vanilla or 1 T.
   Kahlua (coffee liqueur)

In a small saucepan, whisk together cocoa, cornstarch and sugar. Gradually whisk in corn syrup and milk. Bring to a boil, stirring over medium heat. Cook, stirring for 30 to 60 seconds, until thickened. Remove from heat and whisk in oil and vanilla or Kahlua. Let cook and serve at room temperature or chilled.

Yield: about 3/4 cup

Healthy Buffet for Twelve at the Matwiyoffs

* Low Fat Cheese Quesadillas
* Crudites with Low Fat Sauce
  Fatfree pretzel sticks
* Seafood and Rice Casserole
  Raspberry Green Salad (see index)
  Crispy Crust Sourdough
* Lemon Ice Cream Pie with Raspberry Sauce (see index) using
  ice milk for ice cream and low-fat margarine in crust

Janet and Nick Matwiyoff   *Albuquerque*

Janet is responsible for the research and testing of the New Mexico produce and heart healthy recipes in this Raspberry Cookbook. When her husband Nick, who is chairman of Cell Biology at the University of New Mexico's Cancer Center, was advised to cut back on fat and cholesterol, Janet began to be very careful in her cooking. She feels that people are "responsible for their body" and nutrition is most important to people's health. This menu incorporates her favorite recipes with those she tested for the cookbook. The use of nonfat dairy products, including sour cream, cheese and yogurt, make each portion have less than 5 grams of fat. While there is cholesterol in the shellfish, nutritionists are now saying that there is not as much as originally thought, and, if there's a choice between meat and fish, use fish.

♥Low Fat Quesadillas with Homemade Salsa

4 soft 8-inch flour tortillas	1/4 c. canned, diced chiles, or
1 c. shredded 59% fat-reduced	more to taste
mozzarella	1/4 c. chopped green onions

On one half of each tortilla, sprinkle one quarter of the cheese, chile and onion. Fold over tortillas, moistening top and bottom edges with water and pressing down on edges. Gently press down on entire tortilla. Bake at 375° for 10 minutes. Cool on rack for 3 to 5 minutes. Slice with a very sharp knife into 4 to 6 wedges. Serve with Tomato and Cucumber Salsa.

Time: 10 minutes
Temperature: 375°
Servings: 12 to 18

Recipe can easily be doubled and freezes well.

TOMATO AND CUCUMBER SALSA:

1 lg. tomato, diced	1 T. wine vinegar
1 c. cucumber, diced	1 tsp. coriander
2 T. canned, diced green chiles	1 med. clove garlic, minced or
2 T. green onion, minced	through press

Combine all ingredients. Divide and purée half in blender. Add purée to diced half and mix together. Serve at room temperature. Refrigerates well up to 4 days.

Yield: 1 1/2 cups

Crudités with Fat Free Sauce

2 c. bite-sized broccoli flowers	1 1/2 c. slanted, thick celery
1 c. slanted carrot slices	slices

Prepare vegetables and chill well.

FAT FREE SAUCE:	
	3/4 c nonfat sour cream
1 c. nonfat plain yogurt	1 pkg. onion soup mix

Combine yogurt, sour cream and soup mix; allow to stand at room temperature 1/2 hour. Refrigerate in serving dish. Chill platter for vegetables and place sauce and vegetables on it to serve.

Servings: 12

♥Seafood and Rice Casserole

2 (7 1/2 oz.) cans crabmeat,
　well drained
1 Dungeness crab, defrosted,
　cleaned & shelled
3/4 lb. medium shrimp,
　steamed, shelled & deveined
　(about 3 minutes)
2 (2 oz.) lobster tails, steamed
　& shelled (about 7 minutes)
2 T. olive oil
3/4 to 1 lb. mushrooms,
　cleaned & sliced
2 c. green pepper, chopped
2 c. celery, diced

1 c. onion, diced
1 can water chestnuts,
　drained & chopped
Water or broth (optional)
2 c. fat-free mayonnaise
2 tsp. Worcestershire sauce
1 1/2 tsp. salt
1/2 to 1 tsp. black pepper
3 c. white rice, cooked
1 1/2 to 2 c. wild rice, cooked
1/2 to 1 c. sourdough bread
　crumbs
1 T. liquid margarine

Prepare seafood. Flake canned crab over Dungeness, shredding larger chunks. Half (butterfly) cooked shrimp. Slice cooked lobster on the diagonal (don't overcook).

Sauté vegetables and chestnuts in olive oil, adding water or broth by tablespoons if it seems dry. Prepare rices, according to directions. Mix together mayonnaise and Worcestershire sauce; add to cooked rices, tossing lightly. Using large cooking fork, add seafood and toss lightly. Add salt and pepper. Mix only to distribute. Spread into a 2 1/2- to 4-quart casserole. Sprinkle with bread crumbs and drizzle with a little liquid margarine. Bake at 375° for 45 to 60 minutes.

Time: 45 to 60 minutes
Temperature: 375°
Servings: 12

Note: For busy cooks, prepare the Dungeness crab, shrimp and lobster the night before. Chop vegetables and cook wild rice. About 1/2 hour before oven time, cook white rice, sauté vegetables, open canned crab, and proceed with recipe. When serving a larger crowd, don't double the recipe. Make it twice. Use 2 casserole dishes.

This is a very adaptable recipe in which more and less specific shellfish can be used. As it stands, each guest gets 2 to 4 ounces of fish which, together with the recipe and appetizer cheese, is more than adequate protein, plenty of complex carbohydrate, and only a trace of saturated fat. There are 2 to 3 grams fat per serving and lots of fiber from the vegetables and wild rice.

Cookout for Teenagers

* Deep-fried Artichoke Hearts
* Vine Ripened Tomato Slices Vinaigrette
* Broiled Halibut
  Raspberry Marshmallow Pie (see index)

Marsha and Ken Merritt   *Clovis*

Marsha and Ken met at UNM and graduated 25 years ago. Ken is now a dentist in Clovis and Marsha is his hygienist. They have 3 daughters: the eldest graduated from UNM in 1993. Marsha entertains often, especially for her daughters' friends.

Deep-fried Artichoke Hearts

4 c. bread crumbs	1 tsp. pepper
1/2 c. grated Parmesan cheese	20 artichoke hearts, canned or frozen
1 tsp. salt	Lemon butter

Heat deep fat fryer to 350°. Mix bread crumbs, Parmesan cheese, salt and pepper. Coat artichokes with mixture and fry until golden in preheated fryer. It is very important to have the oil hot enough to quick-fry the artichokes. Put in a few at a time to keep the temperature of the oil from dropping. Serve with Lemon Butter.

LEMON BUTTER:

1/2 lb. butter, softened	1 tsp. fresh parsley
3 T. lemon juice	

Combine ingredients and blend well.

Servings: 8 to 10

Vine Ripened Tomato Slices Vinaigrette

4 fresh leaf lettuce leaves, washed

3 lg. vine ripened beefsteak tomatoes

1 red onion, sliced into thin rings

1 c. vinaigrette dressing

Line each salad plate with a lettuce leaf. Core tomatoes and slice each into 4 thick slices. Place 3 slices overlapping on each lettuce leaf. Place several onion rings on top of the tomato slices. Spoon vinaigrette dressing on each salad.

VINAIGRETTE DRESSING:

2 tsp. salt

1 tsp. crushed black pepper

1/4 c. red wine vinegar

3/4 c. salad oil or olive oil

1 T. sugar

1 clove garlic, minced very fine

In a small bowl, dissolve the seasonings in the vinegar and add the minced garlic. Whisk in the oil slowly and incorporate completely. Mix well before serving.

Servings: 4

Broiled Halibut

2 to 2 1/2 lb. halibut, cut into approximately 8 to 10 oz. steaks, 1-inch thick

Salt & pepper to taste

Paprika to taste

Oil

Have coals hot but covered by a coating of white ash. Rinse fish under cold water and pat dry. Sprinkle each fish steak with seasoning and brush well with oil on all sides. Oil the broiler grid well and place the fish steaks over the coals, keeping the grid 4 to 6 inches away from coals. Broil the fish approximately 5 minutes each side, turning only once. When turning the fish, oil the grid again to avoid sticking. Serve immediately.

Time: 10 minutes
Servings: 4 to 6

Charred mesquite wood is best for this recipe, but difficult to find. Charcoal will work as a substitute. Do not use hickory or oak chips as they will overpower the delicate fish flavor.

Supper for My Bridge Club

* Brie Bread Boat
* Spinach Raspberry Salad
* Popovers
* Bridge Club Stew
  Raspberry Crème Brûlée (see index)

Karen Abraham   *Albuquerque*

Karen Abraham is Director of Alumni Relations at the University of New Mexico. Karen has been honored with many community service awards, including the 1992 YMCA's "Woman of the Year" award. She belongs to a bridge club that has been meeting monthly for the past 20 years. Over the years, their supper has grown more important than their bridge playing.

Brie Bread Boat

1 baguette or a long, thin loaf
  of French bread
1/4 c. butter (add 1 clove
  minced garlic or garlic
  powder to taste to make
  garlic butter)

1/2 lb. brie cheese
1/4 lb. garlic & herb spread
  (optional)

Cut the baguette in half lengthwise. Save the top. Scoop out the middle of the bottom so you have a "boat". Brush the inside with melted garlic butter. Slice the brie and generously layer it on top of the garlic butter. (Optional: for a more zesty taste, spread a light layer of garlic herb spread over the butter before adding the layer of brie.) Put bread loaf under broiler until cheese melts. Put top back on bread and serve immediately. (For an extra crusty loaf, put in preheated oven at 425° until cheese melts.) The cut side of the top can be basted with garlic butter and baked under broiler, too.

Servings: Depends on the size of the bread loaf.

This is an easy appetizer people rave about. It can be prepared ahead of time and baked just before serving. The rind of the brie can be removed or left on, depending on personal preference.

Spinach Raspberry Salad

SALAD:

1 or 2 bunches spinach
1 c. fresh raspberries (can add
  other pieces of fruit: cantaloupe,
  honeydew, kiwi, etc.)

1/2 c. coarsely chopped
  macadamia nuts

Rinse and drain spinach. Remove stems. Place spinach leaves on salad plates and sprinkle with raspberries, fruit and nuts.

DRESSING:

2 T. raspberry vinegar
2 T. raspberry preserves
  (raspberry ice cream topping
  can be used instead)

1/3 c. vegetable oil

Combine vinegar and jam in blender or small bowl. Add oil in a thin stream, blending well. Serve immediately. Pour dressing to taste.

Servings: 8

Popovers

2 eggs
1 c. milk
1 c. flour

1/2 tsp. salt
Butter
Raspberry preserves

Break eggs into bowl. Stir milk, flour and salt into eggs with a spoon until just blended. Do not worry about lumps. Pour into 6 generously-buttered custard or popover cups. If custard cups are used, set cups in a muffin pan for secure handling. Pour batter to fill cups 3/4 full. Put into a cold oven and the turn on heat to 450°. Bake exactly 1/2 hour (with no peeking). Remove from oven. Puncture "necks" of popovers in several places with a sharp knife. Return to oven for 10 minutes with the heat off. Remove from cups and serve at once, or cool on rack for later serving. (Reheat on cookie sheet in 350° preheated oven for 5 minutes.) Serve with raspberry preserves.

Time: 30 minutes
Temperature: 450°
Servings: 6

A never-fail, magic recipe, if recipe instructions are followed.

Bridge Club Stew

1 lb. lean beef (sirloin steak suggested)
1/4 c. butter & olive oil (half & half)
Salt & pepper to taste
1 c. red wine
1 1/2 c. water
1 1/2 c. beef broth
1 to 2 tsp. beef bouillon
1 to 2 onions, chopped
Parsley, chopped (the more, the merrier)
1 pinch of thyme
1 bay leaf
1 to 2 cloves garlic
4 med.-sized potatoes, peeled & quartered
5 carrots, thickly sliced
1 sm. can stewed tomatoes, drained
4 stalks celery, cut in medium pieces

Cube beef; dredge with flour and brown rapidly in butter and olive oil. Add salt and pepper to meat as it browns. Pour wine, water, beef broth and beef bouillon to taste onto well-browned meat and keep stirring so as to pick up all the nice "residue" in pan. Add chopped onions, parsley, thyme, bay leaf and garlic to above; simmer until meat is tender (depends on meat—anywhere from 2 to 5 hours). About 45 minutes before serving time, remove bay leaf from meat and add all vegetables, except celery. Add celery last, about 15 minutes before serving.

Servings: 4 to 5 (recipe easy to double)

Stew should be served in soup plates or bowls. This is considered the French way of making stew, a departure from the "thick" variety. Stew tastes even better the second day.

❖

Growing Raspberries in New Mexico
Raspberries not only can be started by bareroot cuttings but also established from tissue-cultured plants. Tissue-cultured plants are generally actively growing plants, 3 to 6 inches high, and grow in individual plugs. These plants are vegetatively propagated in nursery greenhouses from mother-plant cells that have been certified to be virus-free.

Refreshments for an Informal Evening of Poetry

*Elegant Coeur á la Crème
*Sally Seed's Cardiac Crème Brûlee
*Coffee Cream Pie
*Pecan Rum Cake
Gourmet coffee
Variety of liqueurs

Sally Seed *Hobbs*

Sally Seed is a poet and the author of the book of poetry called Bear Songs *published in 1993. She enjoys poetry readings because she "likes the discussion that the poems inspire." When asked to contribute to the cookbook, Sally said, "I think a selection of desserts, coffee and liqueurs would be a fine reward for having endured a poetry reading."*

Elegant Coeur à la Crème

1 lb. cottage cheese	Pinch of salt
2 (8 oz.) pkgs. cream cheese	1 c. heavy cream
2 T. confectioners' sugar	1 pt. raspberries

Line a heart-shaped mold with cheesecloth, leaving an overhang. Press the cottage cheese through a sieve into a large bowl. Beat in the cream cheese, sugar, salt and heavy cream until smooth. Spoon the mixture into the mold. Fold the cheesecloth over the top and press into the mixture slightly. Invert mold and allow to drain on a rack into a pan in the refrigerator overnight. Open cloth. Invert onto plate. Carefully remove cheesecloth. Surround with freshly-washed and drained raspberries.

Servings: 8 to 10

Cardiac Crème Brûlée

1 qt. heavy cream (preferably
    fresh from the dairy)
1 vanilla bean
4 T. sugar

8 egg yolks
Pinch of salt
1 c. light brown sugar

Preheat oven to 350°. In a large saucepan, scald cream with vanilla bean. Do not boil. Add sugar and stir until dissolved.

In a large bowl, beat eggs until lemon-colored. Add the hot cream mixture and salt, stirring as you do. Strain mixture into a shallow 9x9-inch baking dish. Place baking dish into a pan of hot water and bake for 1 hour. Custard is done when a knife comes out clean or nearly clean. It will continue to set as it cools. Refrigerate until completely chilled.

Push brown sugar through a sieve and spread evenly on custard. Place under broiler 2 to 4 minutes, watching very carefully and turning if necessary to caramelize the sugar evenly.

Can be chilled again or served immediately. Crack the sugar with the back of a spoon and serve some with each serving of custard.

Time: 1 hour (baking); 2 to 4 minutes (broiling)
Temperature: 350°
Servings: 6 to 8

Coffee Cream Pie

NUT SHELL:
1 egg white
1/8 tsp. salt
1/4 c. sugar

1 1/2 c. finely chopped New
Mexico pecans

Preheat oven to 400°. Combine egg white and salt; beat until stiff. Gradually beat in sugar until glossy and peaks form. Carefully fold in pecans. Press onto bottom and sides of well-greased 9-inch pie plate. Prick well with fork. Bake 12 minutes.

FILLING:
1/4 lb. or 16 lg. marshmallows
1/4 c. water
1 T. instant coffee granules
1 egg yolk

1 c. heavy cream, whipped;
    or non-dairy whipped
    product
1 T. Kahlua

Continued on following page.

Continued from preceding page.

Combine marshmallows, water and coffee granules over medium heat for 1 minute, stirring constantly, until marshmallows melt. Remove from heat. Beat egg yolk slightly. Add slowly to the hot coffee mixture, beating rapidly. Return saucepan to heat and cook 1 minute. Chill until thick, but not set. Beat slightly and fold in whipped cream and Kahlua. Pour into baked pie shell and refrigerate until serving time.

Time: 12 minutes
Temperature: 400°
Servings: 8

Pecan Rum Cake

CAKE:

1 pkg. yellow cake mix	1/2 c. oil
1 sm. pkg. instant pudding mix	1/2 c. rum
4 eggs	1 1/2 c. chopped New Mexico
1/2 c. cold water	pecans

Preheat oven to 325°. In large bowl, beat cake mix, pudding mix, eggs, water, oil and rum until well blended. Grease and flour a tube pan. Sprinkle chopped pecans on bottom of pan. Pour in the batter. Bake for 1 hour. Cool. Invert onto a plate.

GLAZE:

1/2 stick butter (4 T.)	1 c. sugar
1/4 c. water	3/4 c. rum

Boil together for about 5 minutes. Spoon and pour glaze over the cake until absorbed. Serve with whipped cream, if desired.

Time: 1 hour
Temperature: 325°
Servings: 10 to 12

Very Special Arts Administrator's Dinner with Raspberries

INGREDIENTS:

Go to the Price Club. (If none is near, you may have to starve.) Pass the office supply section quickly. Go directly to the frozen foods. Buy everything in single portion, microwavable packets.

METHOD:

(1) Take your purchase to your home or office (or in those cases where they are one and the same, be sure to find the dirty dishes indicating kitchen facilities).

(2) Do not worry about feeding your family, all relatives have long since given up on you.

(3) If you are lucky, you remember the directions for microwave operation. Otherwise, press any button for 2 minutes.

(4) Avoid upper body injuries by waiting 2 minutes to remove packet.

(5) Fingers are fair game if no fork can be found. Open mouth, chew, swallow, chew.

(6) Now you can breathe, or sleep if necessary.

If you want raspberries, go to the Very Special Raspberry Festival and disregard steps 1 to 6.

Beth Rudolph   *Albuquerque*

Beth Rudolph, Executive Director of Very Special Arts New Mexico, has been a driving force behind the creation and development of the Very Special Raspberry Festival.

Appetizers
& Beverages

"Little Red Riding Hood"
Patricia Jeanette Zagone - Age 6
Nob Hill Elementary, Ruidoso
"Start With the Arts" residency program

Appetizers

Green Chile and Raspberries

1 (4 to 6 oz.) jar green chile
jelly
1 (8 oz.) pkg. cream cheese

1 (10 oz.) pkg. frozen raspberries, thawed
Crackers

Soften jelly in jar for about 30 seconds in microwave or on stove top in hot water. Just before serving, pour it over the block of cream cheese. Cover jelly in swirls with raspberries. Serve on a serving platter with crackers and butter knives for guests to serve themselves.

Serves: 12 to 16

The combination of green jelly and red raspberries would be particularly festive for a Christmas party.

Joy Jeffrey *Albuquerque*

Pickled Green Chile a la Mora

2 c. whole green chile
4 cloves garlic, peeled & sliced
1 c. raspberry vinegar

1 c. sugar
1 tsp. dill seed
1 tsp. mustard seed

Cut the chile into bite-size pieces. Place in a jar with the garlic. In a saucepan place raspberry vinegar, sugar, dill seed, and mustard seed; bring to a boil, stirring to dissolve the sugar. Simmer gently for 5 minutes. Pour over the chile-garlic. Refrigerate. Serve as appetizer with crackers. Also good on scrambled eggs, hamburgers and other sandwiches.

Servings: 12

Best if made at least 3 days in advance. Keeps for several weeks.

Karen Turner *Albuquerque*

Used in the 1991 Raspberry Festival recipe brochure.

Ham/Raspberry/Green Chile Roll-Ups

Spread a thick layer of cream cheese on a thin slice of baked ham. Sprinkle with chopped green chiles and chopped fresh raspberries. Roll and secure with a cocktail-sword toothpick. Slice into bite-sized pieces.

Servings: 1

Joy Jeffrey   *Albuquerque*

Joy Jeffrey is an experimental cook and a collector of cookbooks. In her 500 cookbooks, she will find a recipe and adapt it to her liking. She was a valuable contributor to our cookbook, collecting recipes from restaurants and many interesting New Mexicans. Her name may sound familiar; she was featured in Life *magazine while she was fighting for the release of her husband, Vick, when he was in a Vietnam POW camp.*

Fresh Salsa

(Traditional)

4 to 6 med. red ripe tomatoes, chopped (to make 1 1/2 c.)
1/2 c. minced onion (preferably white)
1/4 to 1/2 c. green chile, hot or mild, chopped
1/4 c. chopped cilantro (fresh coriander)
Pinch of salt
Squeeze of lemon or 1 tsp. vinegar (raspberry is interesting)
Ground black pepper to taste (opt.)
1 clove garlic (opt.)

Combine all ingredients except garlic in a medium-size bowl. If serving salsa within an hour or two, press garlic juice out into tomato mixture. If salsa is holding longer (it is best used within 24 hours), mash clove, put in mixture, and remove just before serving.

Note: The salsa will be more flavorful if the watery seed pulp is squeezed from the tomatoes before they are chopped. In Mexico, the tomatoes are broiled first, adding an extra robust flavor. Tomato juice can be used to make the salsa more "sauce-y".

Yields: Approximately 2 1/2 cups

Marianne Dickinson   *Albuquerque*

Fruit Medley

1/2 cantaloupe	1 c. fresh raspberries
1/2 honeydew melon	6 to 8 sm. clusters of
About 3 lb. watermelon	seedless grapes
2 T. orange-flavored liqueur	

Scrape balls from melons. Combine gently tossed mixture of melon balls in either a scooped out melon half or a clear glass bowl. Sprinkle liqueur and 1 cup fresh raspberries over balls. Garnish plate or tray with grape clusters.

This is a refreshing appetizer for a meal on a hot summer evening. It complements a hot meal such as a New Mexican dinner with red and green chile.

Servings: 10 to 12

Joy Jeffrey   *Albuquerque*

Pineapple Chile Salsa with Raspberries

1 1/2 c. diced fresh pineapple	3 T. minced cilantro
1/4 c. chopped cucumber	3 T. lime juice
1/2 c. chopped red pepper	2 tsp. sugar
1/2 c. chopped onion	Dash of salt
1/4 c. chopped green chile	1 c. whole fresh raspberries

Mix all ingredients together and let stand for at least 1 hour before serving. At the last minute, add fresh whole raspberries.

Servings: 6

The raspberries add a piquancy and beautiful color. Use the salsa with freshly grilled fish, especially Rocky Mountain trout. It may also be used as an appetizer, filling "cups" made of cherry tomatoes, cucumber, or zucchini.

Karen Turner   *Albuquerque*

Karen, the former Executive Director of the Carrie Tingley Hospital Foundation, submitted this recipe for the 1991 Raspberry Festival brochure.

Beverages

Cranberry-Raspberry Sipper

2 c. low-calorie cranberry juice
cocktail, chilled
1 c. frozen loose-pack raspberries

1 c. ice cubes
Mint sprigs (opt.)

In a blender, combine juice cocktail and berries. Cover and blend until almost smooth. Sieve mixture and discard seeds. Return to blender. Add ice cubes; cover. Blend until smooth. Garnish with mint.

Servings: 5

Nonfat yogurt may be added for a breakfast drink. Substitute apple juice for cranberry juice if desired.

Barbara Jones   *Albuquerque*

Celebrity Sundowner
(Health Drink)

6 oz. crushed ice
1/2 banana
1/2 c. raspberries (fresh as
possible)
1/4 cored apple with peel

1 T. raisins
1 T. raw peanuts
1 T. yogurt
1 tsp. honey
1 c. milk (whole or skim)

Blend all ingredients in a blender until smooth.

Servings: 2

Carolyn Whitehill   *Alcalde*

Carolyn is representing the Santa Fe foundation, Santa Maria El Mirador, with her energizing drink recipe.

Raspberry Mint Crush

1/4 c. sugar
1/2 c. fresh mint leaves, lightly
   packed
1 c. boiling water

1 (10 oz.) pkg. frozen raspberries
1 (6 oz.) can frozen lemonade
   concentrate
2 c. cold water

Combine sugar, mint leaves, and boiling water. Let stand 5 minutes. Add raspberries and frozen lemonade concentrate. Stir until thawed. Add 2 cups cold water and stir. Serve over ice.

Servings: 8

Marion Fleck   *Albuquerque*

Party Punch

2 extra-ripe bananas, peeled
1 pt. frozen vanilla yogurt,
   softened
2 firm bananas, peeled

2 c. raspberries
2 liters lemon-lime soda
Mint sprigs

Purée extra-ripe bananas in blender. Add to punch bowl. Stir in yogurt and add sliced bananas and raspberries. Pour in soda. Garnish with mint.

Servings: 14

Carol M. Cherpelis   *Albuquerque*

Raspberry-Ade

2 c. raspberry juice
1 c. orange juice
1/2 c. frozen lemonade

2 c. ice water or carbonated
   water

Mix all ingredients and pour over ice in tall glasses.

Servings: 6

Genevieve Chavez   *Mesilla Park*

Raspberry Shrub

Raspberries
White wine vinegar, to cover

Cold water or ginger ale
Sugar, to taste

Wash the raspberries and put them in a jar, pressing them in slightly. Pour in enough vinegar to cover the berries well. Cover the jar and place in a cool place for a month. Strain the juice into a clean jar and discard the raspberries. Store in the refrigerator until needed.

To serve raspberry shrub, dilute the juice with water or ginger ale and add sugar to taste. Serve in ice-filled glasses for a refreshing summer drink. If large quantities of raspberries are available, the juice can be bottled in sterilized jars to keep without refrigeration.

An old-fashioned recipe, but still good.

Mary Rushton   *Phoenix, AZ (formerly of Gallup)*

Cran-Raz Float and Cran-Raz Soda

1 qt. cran-raspberry drink,
   chilled

1 pt. raspberry sherbet

Thoroughly chill cran-raspberry drink. With small ice cream scoop, put 1 scoop raspberry sherbet in 4 or 6-ounce drink glasses or champagne flutes. Add cran-raspberry drink.

For the Cran-Raz soda, add about 1 ounce bottled club soda to each serving. This is a refreshing palate cooler to accompany spicy foods.

Servings: 8 to 10

Maxine Friedman   *Albuquerque*

Lisa's Raspberry Punch

1 lg. can lemonade concentrate
1 ctn. frozen raspberries or 2 c.
   fresh raspberries

1 (2-liter) btl. lemon-lime
   carbonated drink
Sliced lemons & limes

Mix lemonade 3/4 strength. Add remaining ingredients into a punch bowl and stir. Add ice.

Optional: Serve punch with white wine. Add 1 bottle to punch or serve the bottle alongside the punch bowl.

Servings: 14 to 18

Catherine Cross Maple   *Albuquerque*

Catherine Cross Maple served as director of development for the Very Special Arts New Mexico in 1993. She gave us this recipe in 1991 for the Festival brochure.

Atole de Raspberries

1/2 c. atole flour (blue corn)
1 tsp. cinnamon
2 c. water
3/4 c. sugar
3 c. milk

Dash of vanilla
1 1/2 c. whole raspberries
1 c. sweet cream
3 egg yolks

Mix flour with cinnamon and water. Put in heavy pan to simmer, stirring constantly until thickened. Remove from stove. Dissolve the sugar in the milk and add to hot mixture. Add vanilla and crushed raspberries. Add cream and mix well. Return to heat. Beat in egg yolks, one at a time, beating after each addition. Return to stove. Heat to boiling point. Serve immediately.

Variations: Substitute 8 tablespoons blanched ground almonds for the raspberries. Use strawberries instead of raspberries (a few drops of red food coloring may be added to the drink with the berries).

Servings: 6

Dora Duran and Janet Stein Romero   *Las Vegas (N.M.)*

Dora is a volunteer with the Very Special Arts New Mexico. Janet is the VSA New Mexico District coordinator for the Las Vegas area.

Herbal Drink

2 tsp. raspberry vinegar   1 c. hot water
1 tsp. honey

Mix all ingredients together.

Servings: 1

Alice Blackley   *Albuquerque*

Alice was one of our devoted testers for the cookbook. Recently she was in a herb store in Pennsylvania where the salesperson gave her this recipe. The story was "I used to have a drink of Scotch every night before going to sleep, and now I drink this. It tastes much better!"

Raspberry Brandy

2 gal. ripe raspberries   1 1/2 qt. brandy
1 1/2 lb. sugar

Mash berries to extract juice. Strain through several layers of cheesecloth. Discard solids. Combine juice and sugar; bring to a boil. Reduce heat and simmer juice mixture 3 minutes, stirring constantly. Cool completely. Add brandy and stir well. Pour into attractive bottles. Cork or cap tightly.

Yields: 5 quarts

Phil Lenk   *Albuquerque*

Phil Lenk, pianist and composer, can often be heard playing in Albuquerque at the Rancher's Club in the Hilton Hotel. He also has provided entertainment for the Raspberry Festival. He has completed his fourth album, "Miscelenkeous".

Raspberry Liqueur

Zest from 1 sm. lemon
6 c. fresh raspberries

2 1/2 c. sugar
1 fifth vodka

Combine zest, raspberries, sugar and vodka in 1 gallon jar. Place in a cool dark place. Invert jar daily until sugar is dissolved (approximately 6 days). Allow to stand for 6 weeks. Strain through cheesecloth. Pour into bottles. Cap. After 4 weeks, siphon clear liquid into decorative bottles. The clear glass-type with porcelain tops found in gourmet shops or wine-making supply outlets are nice.

Yields: Approximately 1 quart

Gordon Sanders   *Albuquerque*

Gordon Sanders has been a well-known radio and television personality in New Mexico for 35 years.

Berry Wine

10 lb. ripe berries
1 1/2 pkg. yeast

5 lb. sugar

In a 5-gallon "crock" vessel, place berries and fill with water. Add yeast and sugar; stir well. Let liquid stand for 1 1/2 to 2 months, stirring gently twice a week. In the fermentation of berries, time is the main ingredient. At the end of the 2 months, strain the berries from your newly fermented wine. A cheesecloth or a clean flour sack will do. Bottle as desired.

Rose Archuleta   *Taos Pueblo*

When asked for raspberry recipes that the women would fix in the pueblo, Rose's son Richard answered, "We just ate them". The Taos children would find the wild raspberries and "eat them as quickly as they found them." This recipe usually is made with chokecherries.

Raspberry Fizz

1 (10 oz.) pkg. frozen rasp-
    berries, partially thawed
1/2 c. orange juice

1/2 c. vodka or wine
1 (10 oz.) btl. lemon-lime
    carbonated beverage

Process raspberries and orange juice in blender until smooth. Stir in remaining ingredients. Serve at once over crushed ice.

Servings: 6

June Perovich   *Albuquerque*

John and June Perovich retired in 1985 after serving UNM for 36 years. For the final 3 years, John was UNM's twelfth president.

Raspberry Cream

1 oz. vodka
3/4 oz. Chambord/raspberry
    liqueur

2/3 oz. cream

Fill a rocks glass with ice. Add the vodka and Chambord. Float the cream on top.

Janice and Dennis Bonfantine   *Albuquerque*

In Albuquerque, everyone knows Kelly Liquors as the place to find a very large beverage selection and some of the most helpful folks. Owners Janice and Dennis created some excellent raspberry drinks for the cookbook.

Champagne Berry

1/2 oz. Chambord/raspberry
    liqueur

1/2 oz. kirsch/cherry liqueur
4 oz. champagne

Add kirsch and Chambord to a prechilled champagne glass. Add chilled champagne slowly.

Janice and Dennis Bonfantine   *Albuquerque*

Raspberry Daiquiri

1 1/2 oz. rum	1/2 c. fresh or frozen rasp-
2 oz. sweetened lemon or lime	berries
juice	1/2 tsp. superfine sugar

Pour all ingredients into a blender with 1 cup cracked ice. Blend for 30 seconds and pour into a chilled, large stemmed glass. In place of lemon or lime juice, can use sweet and sour.

Janice and Dennis Bonfantine   *Albuquerque*

Raspberry Joy

1 1/2 oz. white créme de	3 oz. fresh or frozen raspberries
menthe	1 1/2 oz. heavy cream

Puree raspberries in blender with white créme de menthe. Pour into chilled margarita glass. Gently stir in cream. Garnish with shaved white or bitter chocolate.

Servings: 1

Ervin Propes   *Albuquerque*

Ervin Propes, a newcomer to Albuquerque, enjoys creating tasty and creative drinks. When asked to use his ability and use raspberries, he met the challenge well.

Frozen Raspberry Margarita

1/4 c. tequila	2 c. raspberries (or black-
2 T. Triple Sec	berries), frozen or fresh
1/4 c. Margarita mix	1 1/2 c. crushed ice
	1 c. raspberry sorbet or ice

Combine tequila, Triple Sec, Margarita mix and berries in blender. Process until smooth. Add crushed ice and blend. Add raspberry sorbet or ice and blend until slushy. Turn into chilled clear Margarita or champagne glasses. Garnish with a mint leaf and whole berry.

Servings: 4 to 6

Ervin Propes   *Albuquerque*

Notes

Breakfasts,
Breads &
Preserves

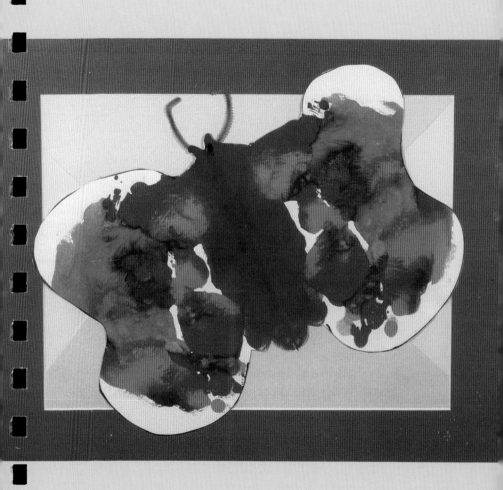

"Butterfly" (Tempera)
Michael Woodall - Age 5
Nob Hill Elementary School, Ruidoso
"Start With the Arts" residency program

Breakfasts

♥A Raspberry Way to Start the Day

1/3 c. oat or bran flakes or
  high vitamin flakes
1/2 c. very high fiber cereal
  (11 to 13 grams per oz.)

1/2 c. individually frozen
  raspberries
2 to 3 T. crunchy wheat &
  barley cereal
6 oz. skim milk

Put the first 2 cereals into bowl and sprinkle with frozen berries. Microwave on MEDIUM for 1 minute. Add third cereal and milk and you have a meal!

This breakfast provides 16 to 17 grams of fiber, nearly half the daily recommended of 27 to 35 grams. It provides 1/3 daily calcium requirements and numerous vitamins and minerals for about 250 calories and essentially no fat.

Janet Matwiyoff   *Albuquerque*

❖

Growing Conditions for Raspberries in the Mora Valley
The altitude of La Cueva is 7100 feet. Summer days are quite warm and nights wonderfully cool. The soil is only slightly alkaline, the water is pure (no salts) and raspberries thrive there.

♥Healthy, Nutty Raspberry Pancakes

1/2 c. prepared biscuit mix
1/4 c. soy milk drink or whole
  milk
1 T. sunflower seeds
1 egg white
1 T. sesame seeds

1 T. walnuts or pecans,
  chopped
1 T. oats
1/4 c. fresh or frozen raspberries
Raspberry preserves & butter
  or nonfat yogurt

Mix above ingredients and stir until smooth. Gently fold in raspberries. Spray medium or large skillet (or griddle) with cooking spray. Heat over medium heat. Divide batter equally and spoon into skillet. Spread until about 5 inches in diameter. Cook until brown. Flip and brown on the other side. Top with butter or yogurt and raspberry preserves.

Pancakes will be thick and cake-like. Can also be eaten with hands. Instead of nuts, granola-type dry cereal can be substitute.

Recipe can easily be doubled.

Servings: 3 per doubled recipe

Jack and Millie Dew Maguire   *Santa Fe*

Swedish Pancakes

3 eggs
1 c. sugar
1 c. flour
1 tsp. baking powder

1/2 c. butter, clarified (see
  index)
1 1/2 c. raspberries, puréed
Confectioners' sugar

Beat together eggs and sugar until thick and lemon-colored. Stir in flour and baking powder. Mix in clarified butter. Pour 1/3 of the batter into a greased skillet. Bake at 425° for 5 to 7 minutes. Repeat this process twice more.

To serve, spread purée between the pancakes and dust top with confectioners' sugar.

Time: 5 to 7 minutes
Temperature: 425°
Servings: 3 to 6

Joan Wax   *Las Cruces*

Breads

Raspberry Muffins

1/4 c. butter or margarine, at
   room temperature
1 lg. egg
1/4 c. packed brown sugar
1/4 c. granulated sugar
1/2 tsp. salt
3/4 c. buttermilk
2 c. all-purpose flour
1/2 tsp. baking soda
1 tsp. ground cinnamon
1 tsp. grated lemon peel
1 c. fresh raspberries

Preheat oven to 375°. In a large bowl, beat butter, egg, sugars, and salt until well blended. Stir in buttermilk; set aside. In a large bowl, stir together flour, baking soda, and cinnamon. Pour egg mixture over dry ingredients and stir to blend. Add lemon peel. Gently fold raspberries into batter. Fill greased muffin cups 2/3 full with batter. Bake for 25 minutes. Remove from oven and immediately turn out onto a wire rack.

Time: 25 minutes
Temperature: 375°
Servings: 12

Beth Rosenstein   *Albuquerque*

Whole Wheat Raspberry Muffins

2/3 c. whole wheat flour
2/3 c. flour
1/3 c. sugar
2 tsp. baking powder
3/4 c. buttermilk
2 eggs, well beaten
2 T. margarine
1 tsp. grated lemon peel
1 c. mashed fresh raspberries
   (or 14 oz. pkg. frozen raspberries)

Combine flours, sugar and baking powder. In another bowl, combine buttermilk, eggs, margarine, and lemon peel. Add this mixture to flour mixture and mix until just moistened. Stir in raspberries. Spoon into lightly greased muffin tins (about 3/4 full). Bake at 375° for 20 minutes.

Time: 20 to 25 minutes
Temperature: 375°
Yield: 12 muffins

Sharon Ball   *Albuquerque*

Raspberry Bran Muffins

2 1/2 c. all-purpose flour
1 3/4 c. sugar
2 tsp. baking powder
1/2 tsp. baking soda
1/2 tsp. salt

2 c. buttermilk
1/2 c. vegetable oil
2 lg. eggs
8 c. bran flakes cereal
1/2 c. raspberry jam

Preheat oven to 350°.

Line muffin tins with paper muffin cups. Combine flour, sugar, baking powder, baking soda, and salt in medium bowl. Whisk buttermilk, oil, and eggs in large bowl to blend. Add dry ingredients and cereal; stir until just blended. Spoon 1/4 cup batter into each muffin cup. Using small spoon, make well in center of each and fill well with 1 teaspoon jam. Spoon remaining batter over each muffin. Bake until tester inserted into centers comes out clean, about 25 minutes. Turn muffins out onto racks; cool slightly. Serve warm or at room temperature.

Time: 25 minutes
Temperature: 350°
Yield: 12

Wyomie Watson   *Albuquerque*

❖

Growing Raspberries in New Mexico
Getting bareroot raspberry cuttings to survive is no easy feat. Root stimulators and liquid gels that attract moisture to the roots help improve getting them established. Root development also occurs faster at cooler soil temperatures, thus spring plantings are encouraged. To prevent wind from drying out the plants, supply windbreaks such as walls or trees on the south and west sides of a raspberry planting.

Orange Scones with Raspberry Filling

3 1/4 c. flour	3 eggs, beaten
1/4 c. sugar	1/2 c. whipping cream
3 to 4 tsp. baking powder	1 T. grated orange peel
1/2 tsp. salt	3 T. raspberry preserves
6 T. margarine or butter	

Heat oven to 425°. Mix flour, sugar, baking powder, and salt. Cut in margarine until mixture resembles coarse crumbs. Beat eggs, cream, and orange peel. Add to flour mixture, mixing just until moistened. Shape dough into a ball. Knead 10 minutes on lightly floured surface. Divide in half. Roll out each half to a 12x6-inch rectangle. Spread one rectangle with preserves. Top with remaining rectangle. Cut into eight 3-inch squares. Cut each in half diagonally. Place on lightly greased cookie sheet. Bake 12 to 14 minutes or until lightly browned. Sprinkle with powdered sugar.

Time: 12 to 14 minutes
Temperature: 425°
Yield: 16 scones

Scones are slightly sweetened biscuits enriched with egg and cream. They are sold throughout England, especially at quaint little tea shops. Scones are delicious in a bread basket at a brunch.

Joy Jeffrey *Albuquerque*

Preserves

Wild Red Raspberry Jelly

About 5 qts. raspberries   1 box Sure-Jell
  (enough to make 4 c. juice.   1/2 tsp. butter
  Wild strawberry juice may   3 (21 oz.) jars or 6 (8 oz.) jars
  be substituted for 1/2 c.)

Squeeze raspberry juice through cheesecloth. Do this about 3 to 4 times to catch all the seeds.

Put 4 cups juice in large pot. Add 1 box Sure-Jell and butter. Stir and boil, then add sugar all at once. Return to boil and cook 5 minutes; then boil hard, 1 minute. Skim off foam. Pour in hot jars 1/8-inch from top. Secure lids. Invert once, then upright.

Yield: 3 (21-ounce) jars or 6 (8-ounce) jars

Joan Graham   *Angel Fire*

Red Raspberry Jam

1 c. red raspberries   2 T. fruit pectin
1 c. + 6 T. white sugar   2 Mason jars with lids, bands

Wash jars, lids and bands. Place jars in 2-quart saucepan, lids in small saucepan. Cover with water. Boil both 10 minutes; drain jars.

Prepare raspberries. Crush in blender 1 minute. Place crushed berries in large saucepan. Add 2 tablespoons fruit pectin to berries. Bring mixture to full rolling boil over very high heat, stirring constantly, using a wooden spoon. Quickly add sugar to berry mixture. Bring back to full rolling boil, stirring constantly, for 1 minute. Remove from heat. Skim off any foam with large metal spoon.

Fill jars immediately to 1/8-inch of tops. Wipe jar rims and threads. Cover quickly with lids. Screw on bands tightly. Invert jars for 5 minutes, then turn upright. After 1 hour, check seals.

Yield: 2 half-pints

Kathy Leger   *Las Vegas*

Kathy works with Very Special Arts in Las Vegas, New Mexico.

Canned Raspberries

Place raspberries in a quart jar. Boil 1 1/2 cups sugar with 1 cup water until it hairs. Pour this over the berries. Screw on the top and set in boiling water overnight.

Note: From my grandmother's cookbook, *Washington Women's Cookbook*, published by the Washington Equal Suffrage Association, in 1909. Isn't that terrific!

Pam Darnell   *Prairie Village, KS*

Mock Raspberry Preserves

4 c. tomato pulp
4 c. sugar

1 (6 oz.) (lg.) box red raspberry gelatin

Skin tomatoes. Squeeze out water and mash. The yield should equal 4 cups. Bring pulp to boil. Add sugar and bring to rolling boil for 10 minutes. Add gelatin and stir to dissolve. If tomatoes are used late in the season and are too watery, add 2 or 3 teaspoons of extra gelatin. Put in sterilized jars.

Yield: 4 pints jam

Donna tells us: "This is an old recipe which was given to me when I had too many tomatoes in my garden and did not know what to do with them. It is very sweet. However, it is an interesting conversation piece to use at special times."

Donna Peck   *Albuquerque*

Green Tomato Raspberry Jelly

5 c. drained green tomato juice
4 c. sugar

2 sm. pkg. or 1 lg. pkg. raspberry gelatin

Grind enough tomatoes to make 5 cups juice and drain for 11 minutes. Put juice and sugar in pan. Simmer for 10 minutes. Add raspberry gelatin; stir. Bring to a boil. Place in jars and seal.

Yield: 5 jars jelly

This recipe comes from the M. Baca's family farm. This is what was done with the tomatoes that could not ripen before the first freeze.

M. Baca   *Las Cruces*

Raspberry Chile Chutney

1/4 c. orange juice	3/4 tsp. curry powder
1/4 c. raspberry vinegar	3/4 c. golden raisins
1 c. sugar	1 cinnamon stick
1/4 c. orange zest (peel) in	1/4 c. diced green chile
julienne strips	3 lb. oranges, peeled, white
1/4 c. crystallized ginger	removed, & cut up
1/2 tsp. red hot sauce	4 c. fresh raspberries
1 clove garlic, peeled	

Heat to boiling, orange juice, vinegar, sugar and orange zest. Stir to dissolve sugar. Add ginger, red hot sauce, garlic, curry, raisins, cinnamon stick and chile. Add chopped oranges and raspberries, stirring gently (the raspberries are rather fragile and may break). Cool. Remove garlic and cinnamon stick. Refrigerate up to 6 weeks.

Yield: 1 1/2 quarts

Idros Howard   *Albuquerque*

Idros submitted this recipe for the Raspberry Festival brochure in 1991.

Raspberry Fruit Leather

2 1/2 qt. whole raspberries	Margarine (for greasing
1 c. sugar	cookie sheets)
1/4 to 1/2 c. water	Cornstarch

Have at hand a knife or spatula, large kettle, blender, cookie sheets, wire racks, wax paper and oven thermometer. Choose fully ripe fruits; wash well. Put raspberries into a large kettle. Add sugar and enough water to prevent sticking. Heat just until boiling. Remove from heat. Blend several batches in blender until smooth. Purée should be about the consistency of apple butter. If thinner, return to kettle and simmer until thicker; cool slightly.

Lightly grease cookie sheets. Evenly spread the purée about 1/4-inch thick on the sheets. Dry at 120° in oven until the leather is firm to the touch and will come off the sheet in 1 piece. Put leather on wire racks and allow to cool completely. Sift a small amount of cornstarch on each side to prevent sticking. Lay the fruit leather on a strip of wax paper. Roll it up and store in a plastic bag in a cool, dark place.

Yield: 2 to 3 cookie trays, depending on size of tray.

Carol Beserra   *Albuquerque*

Soups, Salads, & Dressings

"Three Bears"
Ashley Rhoten - Age 6
Nob Hill Elementary, Ruidoso
"Start With the Arts" residency program

Soups

Fruit Soup

1 pt. raspberries	1 pt. sour cream
Sugar to taste (omit if frozen, sweetened berries are used)	1 to 2 c. champagne to dilute to desired consistency

Purée all ingredients in a blender and serve in stemmed glasses.

Servings: 4 to 6

Sally Seed   *Hobbs*

Cold Raspberry Soup with Port

4 (10 oz.) pkg. frozen raspberries, thawed	4 short cinnamon sticks
2 c. port wine	2 tsp. cornstarch
	1/2 c. water

In a 3-quart saucepan, over medium heat, heat raspberries, port and cinnamon sticks to boiling. Reduce heat to low and simmer 10 minutes. In a measuring cup, mix cornstarch with water. Slowly stir into soup. Cook until thickened, stirring constantly. Remove cinnamon sticks before serving.

Servings: 4 to 6

Naomi Mosley   *Albuquerque*

Raspberry Rosé Soup

1 pt. fresh raspberries	1/3 c. rosé (or white Zinfandel) wine
1/4 c. honey	1/2 c. half & half
8 oz. nonfat yogurt	1/2 c. skim milk

Place all ingredients in blender or food processor. Whirl until thoroughly blended. Serve chilled. Garnish with whole raspberries and mint leaves.

Servings: 6 to 8

Sheila Harris   *Albuquerque*

Raspberry and Currant Soup

1 c. red raspberries	Sugar
1 c. red currants	2 T. cornstarch
1 qt. cold water	Pinch of nutmeg
1/2 lemon, juice & rind	

Cover berries and currants with the water. Bring slowly to a boil. Let boil a few minutes to extract juice, then strain. There should be a quart of liquid. Add juice and grated rind of the lemon. Sweeten to taste. Add cornstarch moistened with a little cold water. Cook until thickened, stirring constantly. Add nutmeg. Serve cold or warm.

Servings: 6

This recipe comes from a 60-year-old cookbook belonging to Debra's mother.

Debra Thornton   *Albuquerque*

Salads

Raspberry Spinach Salad

2 lb. fresh spinach	2 pt. fresh raspberries

Wash and dry spinach. Remove stems and tear into pieces. Wash and dry raspberries.

To serve, arrange spinach and raspberries on chilled plates. Drizzle dressing over top.

DRESSING:

1/3 c. sugar	1/2 c. safflower oil
1 1/2 tsp. minced onion	3 to 4 T. cider vinegar
1/4 tsp. paprika	2 T. sesame seeds
1/4 tsp. Worcestershire sauce	1 T. poppy seeds

Whisk or blend together sugar, onion, paprika, and Worcestershire sauce. Gradually add oil and vinegar in a steady stream until well blended. Stir in sesame and poppy seeds.

Servings: 6 to 8

Carol Cherpelis   *Albuquerque*

Steve Schiff's Spinach Raspberry Salad

6 c. spinach leaves, separated
1 c. fresh raspberries, divided
1 sm. Bermuda onion, thinly
   sliced
1 c. macadamia nuts,
   chopped & divided
1 avocado, peeled & sliced
1/2 c. cilantro leaves,
   chopped

In large bowl, combine spinach, raspberries, onion, nuts, avocado, and cilantro. Reserve a few raspberries and nuts for garnish.

DRESSING:
1/2 c. sesame oil
1/4 c. raspberry vinegar
1 T. seedless raspberry jam
Salt & pepper

In a small bowl, mix oil, vinegar, jam, salt, and pepper. Pour dressing over salad and toss gently. Garnish with reserved raspberries and nuts. Serve immediately.

Servings: 6 to 8

The Honorable Steven Schiff   *Washington, D.C.*

Steven Schiff is the United States Congressman for the 1st District of New Mexico. He is a loyal supporter of the Very Special Raspberry Festival.

"Thank you for asking me to contribute to a cookbook that will be part of the annual Raspberry Festival that benefits Carrie Tingley Hospital and Very Special Arts. This event is one of the most looked forward to happenings of the summer. I wish you every success!!"

Raspberry Green Salad

1 head romaine or green leaf lettuce	Fresh raspberries for garnish (opt.)
2 (10 1/2 oz.) cans mandarin oranges, drained	1 avocado, sliced
15 cherry tomatoes, quartered	2/3 c. toasted almonds
1 small jicama root, peeled and julienned	1/3 c. chopped fresh basil
	1 mango, cut in sm. pieces

Layer all ingredients in glass or Lucite bowl for best color display. Toss just before serving with Raspberry Vinaigrette.

RASPBERRY VINAIGRETTE:	1 tsp. white pepper
1 (12 oz.) can cran-raspberry frozen juice concentrate	2 c. red wine vinegar
1 (16 oz.) jar seedless raspberry jam	2 tsp. minced fresh garlic
	1/2 tsp. salt
	2 to 4 c. safflower oil

Process all ingredients except oil until smooth in processor or blender. Divide in 4 parts. Freeze 3 parts in sealed freezer bags. (They will keep in freezer indefinitely.) Slowly add 1 cup safflower oil to remaining part in processor. (Leftover mixed salad dressing will keep in a covered jar in the refrigerator for at least a week.)

To use a frozen portion, defrost. Put in blender and drizzle in 1/2 to 1 cup safflower oil.

Note: You may vary the amount of lettuce. Do not substitute the safflower oil. It has a distinctive taste that glorifies the fruit.

Servings: 8 to 10

Bobbie Engle   *Placitas*

Bobbie Engle has spent hundreds of hours at the computer typing, retyping and retyping again the recipes for the cookbook. Bobbie is new to Albuquerque. She is so pleased to have made so many new friends through their recipes. (This was one of the testing committee's favorite recipes. They all wanted a copy of it immediately.)

Raspberry Gelatin Supreme

1 (3 oz.) pkg. red gelatin
Water (as directed on pkg.)
1/2 c. sugar

1 (11 oz.) can crushed pineapple
1 c. finely chopped celery
1 lg. bag frozen raspberries

Prepare gelatin as directed on the package. Add sugar to hot water so that it will dissolve. Add cold water. Add pineapple, chopped celery, and frozen raspberries; mix gently. Place in refrigerator. Stir occasionally so the added ingredients will be blended throughout the gelatin without crushing the fruit.

Variation: Add chopped pecans or walnuts. Fold in whipped cream, or add marshmallows, when cool.

Servings: 10 to 12

Ann Palmer   *Kirkland*

Ann Palmer is the principal of the Ruth N. Bond Elementary School in Kirkland, N.M.

Raspberry Lemonade Salad

2 (3 oz.) boxes raspberry
gelatin
1 c. boiling water
1 (10 to 12 oz.) pkg. frozen
raspberries

6 oz. frozen lemonade
1 c. heavy cream, whipped (or
use whipped topping)

Add gelatin to boiling water to dissolve. Stir in frozen raspberries and lemonade. Chill until partially set. Fold in whipped cream. Pour into a 9x9-inch pan or other mold. Chill until firm.

Note: Using raspberry lemonade makes the salad a pleasing deep pink.

Servings: 8 to 10

Jane Swift   *Albuquerque*

Raspberry Marshmallow Salad

1 pkg. red raspberry-flavored
   gelatin
1 pt. rinsed, fresh raspberries
1 c. crushed pineapple, well
   drained

1 1/4 c. hot water
8 oz. sour cream
1 (6 1/4 oz.) bag miniature
   marshmallows

Mix gelatin with water until dissolved. Add raspberries and mix. Drain pineapple, saving the juice, and add pineapple to the mixture. Pour mixture into an 8x12-inch Pyrex pan and put in refrigerator to set.

Before serving salad, put 1 cup of sour cream into a medium-size bowl. Add 2 cups miniature marshmallows and the juice from the pineapple. Let stand until marshmallows have absorbed all the liquid, then spread over the gelatin salad. Garnish and serve.

F. Leroy Pacheco   *Albuquerque*

Leroy Pacheco is a former Executive Director of the Albuquerque Hispano Chamber of Commerce.

Raspberry Aspic

5 c. mixed vegetable juice
3 (3 oz.) pkg. raspberry gelatin
6 T. mild horseradish
1 cucumber, sliced for garnish

1/2 to 1 avocado, peeled,
   pitted, sliced for garnish
Parsley sprigs for garnish
Mayonnaise or salad dressing
   for garnish

In large saucepan, heat vegetable juice. Add gelatin and horse-radish. Stir until gelatin is dissolved. Pour into a greased 6-cup ring mold. Chill until set. Remove from mold. Garnish with cucumber, avocado, and parsley. Serve with mayonnaise or salad dressing in the center of the ring.

Servings: 10 to 12

Even those who are not fans of tomato aspic will love this!!

Sandy Eastham   *Albuquerque*

Fruit and Cottage Cheese Mold with Lemon French Dressing

2 tsp. unflavored gelatin	Lettuce or other greens
3 T. canned pineapple juice	Sliced pineapple
2 1/2 c. cottage cheese	Raspberries

Soften gelatin in pineapple juice and dissolve over hot water. Stir into cottage cheese. Pour into 1 large or 6 individual oiled molds and chill until firm. Remove from mold. Garnish individual mold servings with sliced pineapple and raspberries. Use fruit to fill the center of 1 large mold. Serve with Lemon French Dressing.

Servings: 6

LEMON FRENCH DRESSING:	1/2 tsp. salt
1/2 c. olive oil or salad oil	Dash of cayenne pepper
1/2 c. lemon juice	2 T. sugar or honey

Combine all ingredients and shake well before using.

Yield: 1 cup

I. Gene Jones   *Albuquerque*

I. Gene Jones is president of the Albuquerque chapter of Links, an African-American women's service organization.

Raspberry Cheese Ball Salad

1 (10 oz.) pkg. frozen raspberries	1 (3 oz.) pkg. cream cheese, softened
1 (3 oz.) pkg. raspberry gelatin	1/4 c. chopped New Mexico pecans (or walnuts)
1 c. boiling water	Lettuce leaves

Thaw raspberries and drain juice. Add water to make 3/4 cup liquid. Mix gelatin with 1 cup boiling water. When dissolved, add 3/4 cup raspberry liquid and refrigerate until slightly thickened. Form softened cream cheese into small balls and roll in nuts. Add to the slightly thickened gelatin. Pour into an attractive quart mold and refrigerate until set. Unmold and serve on a bed of lettuce.

Servings: 8

Joyce Weitzel   *Corrales*

Raspberry Melon Bowl with Lemon Mayonnaise Dressing

RASPBERRY MELON SALAD BOWL:

1 cantaloupe	Lettuce
1/2 honeydew	1 pt. red raspberries
1/2 clove garlic	

All melons should be served very cold. The melon pulp may be shaped into balls with a French vegetable cutter, diced, or scooped out with a large spoon. Toss fruit in dressing; chill. Rub bowl with garlic. Line with lettuce leaves and arrange tossed, chilled fruit on lettuce.

LEMON MAYONNAISE DRESSING:

1 egg yolk	1/4 c. olive or salad oil
1/4 c. lemon juice	1/2 tsp. salt
2/3 c. sweetened condensed milk	1 tsp. dry mustard

Beat well until mixture thickens. Add 1/4 cup more lemon juice for a more tart flavor. Yields 1 cup.

Servings: 6

Dorothy Posey   *Albuquerque*

Strawberries with Raspberry Compote

1/4 c. sugar	1 (10 to 12 oz.) pkg. frozen
1 pt. fresh strawberries, hulled	raspberries
& cleaned	2 T. cognac (or to taste)

Add sugar to strawberries. Refrigerate for an hour or longer. Put raspberries through a food mill. Just before serving, stir raspberries into strawberries. Add cognac and serve. If desired, use as a sauce over vanilla ice cream.

Servings: 4 to 6

Dan True   *Albuquerque*

Dan True is the author of Flying Free, *the first English language book to be purchased by, and published in, China in 50 years. His new book,* Hummingbirds of North America *was published in 1993 by University of New Mexico Press.*

Frozen Summer Fruit Salad with Pastel Fruit Mayonnaise

1/2 c. sliced raspberries	1 tsp. unflavored gelatin
1/2 c. sliced canned pineapple	1 T. cold water
1/2 c. diced orange segments	4 tsp. drained honey
1/2 c. diced bananas	2/3 c. heavy cream, whipped
2 tsp. lemon juice	Lettuce

Combine all fruits with lemon juice; chill. Soften gelatin in cold water. Dissolve over hot water and add to honey and fruit. Fold whipped cream into fruit mixture and freeze in refrigerator tray 3 hours or until firm. Cut into squares and serve on lettuce.

An alternate method is to freeze in sealed baking powder cans. Before serving, unmold, slice and serve. Place each round of frozen salad on a lettuce leaf. Top with slice of avocado and garnish center with Pastel Fruit Mayonnaise.

Pastel Fruit Mayonnaise: Add raspberry juice or cooked red raspberry purée to mayonnaise recipe below.

MAYONNAISE:	2 egg yolks
1 tsp. salt	1 pt. olive oil or salad oil
1 tsp. dry mustard	1/8 c. cider vinegar
Dash of cayenne	1/8 c. tarragon vinegar

Combine salt, mustard, and cayenne with egg yolks in a mixing bowl. Beat together until stiff. Beat oil into the mixture 1 drop at a time at first, then more rapidly. Always keep the mixture stiff. When it begins to thicken, add a bit of vinegar. Alternate oil and vinegar until blended. Yields 1 1/2 cups.

Servings: 8

Moseller Young   *Albuquerque*

Dressings

Raspberry Glaze Dressing

1/2 c. walnut oil
1/2 c. balsamic vinegar
4 T. honey
1 pt. whole fresh raspberries,
   gently washed & drained

1 T. poppy seeds
1/2 c. piñon nuts (pine nuts)
   or slivered or sliced
   almonds

Combine walnut oil, balsamic vinegar, and honey; whisk until evenly blended. Add whole raspberries, piñon nuts, and poppy seeds, and quickly whisk to a smooth texture.

Yield: 2 cups, serves 6 to 8

This dressing is very good with salads of cold, fresh whole spinach leaves or salad greens.

Jim and Terri Cole   *Albuquerque*

Terri Cole is Executive Director of the Greater Albuquerque Chamber of Commerce. Jim is an oral surgeon. Terri and Jim created this recipe together.

Raspberry-Lemon Vinegar

3 c. fresh raspberries
1 lemon, skin washed

4 c. white wine vinegar (5%
acidity)
1/2 c. sugar

Rinse raspberries. Dry on paper towels. Place in a 6-cup jar. Using a vegetable peeler, remove rind of lemon in long single strip. Add to jar of berries; set aside.

Combine vinegar and sugar in a saucepan; Bring almost to a boil over low heat, stirring constantly, until sugar melts. Pour hot vinegar over berries. Cover jar tightly. Let stand for 48 hours. Remove lemon rind. Strain vinegar through several layers of cheese-cloth to remove berries. Discard berries.

Store vinegar in jars with airtight lids in a cool, dark place up to 6 months. Serve over salad greens.

Yield: 5 cups

Judith R. Harris   *Albuquerque*

Judith is Executive Director of the Sickle Cell Council of New Mexico.

❖

Pruning Raspberries
All canes of everbearing raspberries can be pruned in winter to ground level. Biennial cane varieties such as "Latham" produce vegetative canes one summer that produce fruit the following summer. These varieties require selective pruning, removing canes that have fruited from those that will fruit the next summer.

Raspberry Salad Dressing and Marinade

1 1/2 c. vegetable oil
1/4 c. + 1 T. balsamic vinegar
1/4 c. light soy sauce
1 tsp. Worcestershire sauce
6 T. raspberry jam or 1/3 c. crushed ripe raspberries

1/4 tsp. dry mustard
1/4 tsp. garlic powder
1/2 tsp. hot red chile powder
2 tsp. fresh grated ginger

Pour ingredients into 2-cup container with a tight-fitting lid and shape vigorously. Refrigerate and store for 24 hours before using. It will keep in the refrigerator for up to 2 weeks.

Yields 2 cups

This is a wonderful salad dressing to spice up even the simplest salad. (You may want to toss in a few choice raspberries or nasturtium flowers for color.) It is great on bitter lettuces. It is also a good chicken marinade. Marinate skinless chicken pieces for at least 12 hours in the refrigerator.

Mary Sharp Davis   *Albuquerque*

Mary Sharp Davis is an artist known for her interesting use of mixed media.

Poppy Seed Dressing

1/2 c. Salman Ranch Raspberry Vinegar
1/4 c. honey or sugar
2 tsp. salt
1 tsp. English-style dry mustard

1 T. poppy seeds
1 c. olive or vegetable oil
1/3 c. water
Pepper to taste
1 T. celery seed, if desired, for a more robust flavor

Whisk together all ingredients except oil until honey dissolves. Dribble oil while whisking until mixture is emulsified. Chill covered for 3 hours, and whisk again to recombine before using. Serve dressing over sliced strawberries, apples, plums, nectarines, or any fruit, or fruit combination of your choice.

Yields about 1 3/4 cups

Salman Family   *La Cueva*

Main Dishes
& Vegetables

"Nick, Denise, and Bobby"
Elroy Robinson - Age 12
Mesa Middle School, Roswell
Elroy Robinson was the New Mexico representative for the 200th Anniversary White House project

Main Dishes

Chicken with Raspberry Cream Sauce

2 whole boneless, skinless
chicken breasts (about 1 lb.)
2 T. sweet butter
1/4 c. finely chopped yellow
onion
4 T. raspberry vinegar
1/4 c. chicken stock or
chicken broth

1/4 c. heavy cream or crème
fraîche (below)
1 T. canned, crushed
tomatoes, seedless if you wish
16 raspberries
Raspberry juice to
taste (opt.)

Cut each chicken breast into halves along the breastbone line. Flatten each breast half in your palm. Melt the butter in a large skillet. Raise the heat. Add the filets and cook for about 3 minutes per side, or until they are lightly browned. Remove from the skillet and set aside.

Add the onions to the pan and cook, covered, over low heat, until they are tender, about 15 minutes. Add the vinegar; raise the heat and cook, uncovered, stirring occasionally, until vinegar is reduce to a syrupy spoonful. Whisk in the chicken stock, heavy cream or crème fraîche, and crushed tomatoes; simmer for 1 minute. Return filets to the skillet and simmer them gently in the sauce, basting often, until they are just done and the sauce has been reduced and thickened slightly, about 5 minutes. Do not overcook. Remove filets with a slotted spoon and arrange on a heated serving platter.

Add the raspberries to the sauce in the skillet and cook over low heat for 1 minute. Do not stir the berries with a spoon, merely swirl them in the sauce by shaking the skillet. If desired, add raspberry juice to taste to the sauce. Pour sauce over the filets and serve.

CRÈME FRAÎCHE:
1 c. heavy cream   1 c. dairy sour cream

Whisk heavy cream and sour cream together in a bowl. Cover loosely with plastic wrap and let stand in the kitchen or other

Continued on following page.

Continued from preceding page.

reasonably warm spot overnight, or until thickened. In cold weather, this may take as long as 24 hours. Cover and refrigerate for at least 4 hours, after which the crème fraîche will be quite thick. The tart flavor will continue to develop as the crème fraîche sits in the refrigerator.

Servings: 4

David Hathaway   *Las Cruces*

♥Chicken Breasts with Raspberry Marinade

MARINADE:

3 c. fresh or frozen	3/4 c. olive oil
raspberries (unsweetened	2 bay leaves
if frozen)	2 tsp. herbs de Provence
1 c. raspberry vinegar	3 T. balsamic vinegar

In a small saucepan, combine raspberries and raspberry vinegar. Bring to a boil and boil for 1 minute. Remove from heat and add olive oil, bay leaves, herbs, and balsamic vinegar. Cool.

CHICKEN:

6 boneless, skinless	Salt & freshly ground
chicken breasts	pepper to taste

Place chicken in nonreactive bowl. Pour marinade over chicken. Add salt and pepper. Marinate in refrigerator at least 6 hours or overnight.

Grill over hot coals (about 3 to 4 minutes a side). Serve immediately.

Tabouleh makes a nice accompaniment.

Kathleen Stewart Howe   *Corrales*

Kathleen Stewart Howe is a photohistorian who lives in Corrales, New Mexico. She is the author of Felix Teyvard: Calotypes of Egypt, *published in 1992.*

Chicken Melba

RASPBERRY VINEGAR:

1 pt. white wine, champagne vinegar or white wine vinegar

1 qt. raspberries, crushed

Mix in a jar and allow to stand 3 days. Then strain and pour into clean bottles.

CHICKEN:

1 sealable plastic bag	1/8 tsp. salt
4 chicken breasts, skinned & split	1/2 tsp. Dijon mustard
	2 T. raspberry vinegar
1/2 tsp. sugar	3 T. oil

Place chicken breasts in plastic bag. Blend and pour over chicken: sugar, salt, mustard, vinegar, and oil. Close bag and shake. Marinate in refrigerator for 1 hour or more, turning bag occasionally.

SAUCE:

10 to 12 oz. fresh or frozen raspberries	1/8 tsp. salt
	1 T. cornstarch
1/4 c. jellied cranberry sauce	1 T. chicken marinade
2 T. sugar	1 T. water

Force raspberries through fine strainer. Discard seeds. In a 1-quart saucepan, blend with cranberry sauce; bring to a boil, and cook until cranberry sauce melts. In a small measuring cup, mix sugar, salt, and cornstarch. Blend well with marinade and water. Add to raspberry-cranberry mixture. Bring to a boil, stirring constantly, over medium heat. Reduce heat and simmer 2 minutes.

PREPARATION:

2 T. oil	8 canned peach halves

Preheat oven to 325°.

Remove chicken from marinade and drain on paper towels. Reserve marinade. Use a shallow iron fry pan or flame-proof serving dish large enough to place chicken in a single layer. Sear chicken on each side in 2 tablespoons oil until brown, about 2 minutes on each side. Reduce heat to medium; add 2 tablespoons marinade and simmer for 4 minutes, turning occasionally.

Continued on following page.

Continued from preceding page.

Place 8 canned peach halves on top of chicken. Baste with pan juices. (If this is done in a fry pan, you can at this point place in an oven-proof baking-serving dish and add peaches.) Bake 10 minutes. Baste once with pan juices. Spoon hot sauce over chicken. Leave peaches uncovered. Pass remaining sauce.

Temperature: 325°
Time: 10 minutes
Servings: 4

Susan Lucksted   *Montezuma*

Susan has been part of the Artists in Residence Program for Very Special Arts New Mexico.

Chicken with Raspberry Vinegar

3 T. butter
6 chicken breast halves,
   skinned & cut in half
1/4 c. flour
Salt & ground pepper
1 clove garlic, minced
2 shallots or 2 green onions,
   chopped fine

1 1/2 c. sliced mushrooms
1/4 c. raspberry vinegar
1/2 c. chicken stock
1/2 c. heavy cream
Salt & pepper to taste
Mint leaves

In a large skillet, heat butter. Dust chicken lightly with flour and season with salt and pepper. Sauté chicken on both sides until golden. Remove from pan and set aside.

Remove all but 2 tablespoons of oil from pan. Sauté garlic, onion, and mushrooms until onion is soft. Discard remaining oil. Deglaze pan by adding raspberry vinegar and chicken stock. Add chicken; cover and simmer about 30 minutes, or until chicken juices run clear when pierced with a fork. Remove to heated plate and cover with foil to keep warm.

Bring sauce to a boil and simmer until sauce thickens. Add cream and reduce again, about 4 minutes. Salt and pepper to taste. Serve chicken on rice; pour sauce over chicken. Garnish with mint leaves.

Servings: 4 to 6

Beth Rosenstein   *Albuquerque*

♥Chicken and Raspberry Spinach Salad

DRESSING:

1/4 c. raspberry vinegar or
  white wine vinegar
2 T. salad oil
1 T. honey

1/2 tsp. finely shredded
  orange peel
1/4 tsp. pepper
1/8 tsp. salt

Combine vinegar, salad oil, honey, orange peel, pepper, and salt in a small, screw-top jar. Cover and shake well. Chill until needed.

SALAD:

3 med. skinless, boneless
  chicken breast halves, cut
  into thin, 2-inch strips
1/4 c. orange juice
8 to 10 c. torn, fresh spinach
  leaves or assorted greens
1 c. fresh raspberries

1 papaya, peeled, seeded
  & cut into thin slices, or
2 med. nectarines or peaches,
  pitted & cut into thin slices
Cabbage leaves for 4 plates
  (opt.)

In a microwave-safe 2-quart casserole, combine the chicken, 1/4 cup water, and the orange juice. Micro-cook, covered, on 100% POWER (HIGH) for 4 to 6 minutes, or until the chicken is tender and no longer pink. Drain, discarding the cooking liquid. Cool chicken slightly.

In a large bowl, combine warm chicken and spinach. Add dressing and raspberries; toss gently. Line dinner plates with cabbage, if desired. Divide salad with several papaya, peach, or nectarine slices, arranging them in a fan. Serve immediately.

Servings: 4 main dish salads

Marsha Dompreh   *Albuquerque*

Picking Raspberries
The quickest, safest, and easiest way to pick is the old fashioned way. Take a pail and tie it around your waist with an old belt. This way, both hands are free, and pail is held steady. One hand can pick while the other gently lifts the cane to expose berries on the underside. Many pickers forget to look below, in between, and around the most obvious berries!

Black Bean Chicken Salad with Raspberry Dressing

2 cans black beans
4 chicken breasts, skinned
  & boned

1 can chicken broth

Drain beans well, but do not rinse. Cook chicken breasts gently in chicken broth. Cool chicken and cut in large pieces; add to beans. Set aside.

DRESSING:

1/2 c. vegetable or olive oil
  (or use half and half)
1/4 c. raspberry vinegar
1/2 tsp. salt
1/4 tsp. freshly ground black
  pepper

1/4 tsp. ground ginger
1/4 tsp. Dijon mustard
1 egg yolk
1 sm. can green chile,
  chopped
1 pt. raspberries (for garnish)

Combine all dressing ingredients in a quart jar and shake thoroughly to mix. Add green chile and shake again. Pour over beans and chicken. Chill. Serve over green lettuce leaves. Garnish with fresh raspberries.

Servings: 8 to 10

Joy Jeffrey　　　　　　　　　　　　　　　　　　　　*Albuquerque*

Medicinal Use of Raspberries
The medicinal use of the raspberry plant is fascinating. The raspberry leaves have long been used as a remedy for cramping. It is commonly used as a "woman's tonic" when a tea made from the leaves is drunk cold. A tincture made from the leaves is used as a mild astringent.

♥Northwestern Chicken Salad

RASPBERRY VINAIGRETTE:

1/4 c. pear nectar
2 T. salad oil
2 T. raspberry vinegar
(or white wine vinegar)

1/2 to 1 tsp. Dijon-style
mustard
1 tsp. sesame oil
1/8 tsp. pepper

Combine all ingredients in a jar. Cover and shake well. Store in the refrigerator for up to 2 weeks.

SALAD:

2 boneless, skinless chicken
breast halves (about 8 oz.)
6 to 8 whole strawberries
1 pear, cored & sliced
8 to 10 asparagus spears

8 to 10 whole pecan halves,
toasted (opt.)
Lettuce leaves
4 c. shredded mixed greens
(such as iceberg or Boston)
2 T. chopped sweet onion

Rinse chicken and pat dry. In a medium bowl, combine chicken with 1/2 of the vinaigrette. (Reserve balance for salad dressing.) Cover. Marinate for 30 minutes in the refrigerator. Drain. Reserve marinade.

Grill chicken on an uncovered grill directly over medium-high coals for 15 to 18 minutes, or until no longer pink. Turn once during grilling. Brush with reserved marinade last 5 minutes of grilling. (Or, place chicken on an unheated rack of a broiler pan. Broil 4 to 5 inches from heat about 9 minutes, until no longer pink. Turn once and brush with reserved marinade.) Discard any remaining marinade.

In a medium saucepan, cook asparagus, uncovered, in a small amount of boiling water for 6 to 8 minutes, or until crisp-tender.

Slice each chicken breast crosswise into 6 to 8 pieces. Line 2 plates with lettuce leaves. Divide shredded greens between plates. Top with chicken, asparagus, onion, strawberries, and pear. Top with reserved raspberry vinaigrette. Sprinkle with pecans, if desired.

Servings: 2

Grilled duck breast could be substituted in this recipe.

Zenobia McMurry   *Albuquerque*

♥Broiled Turkey with Raspberry Sauce

1 lb. boneless turkey breast
   steaks
2 tsp. lemon juice

2 T. water
2 tsp. soy sauce

Place turkey on a rack in an unheated broiler pan. Combine lemon juice, water, and soy sauce. Brush turkey with lemon mixture. Broil 5-inches from heat for 6 minutes. Turn and broil about 6 minutes more, or until tender. Brush occasionally with lemon mixture.

SAUCE:
10 oz. frozen red raspberries,
   thawed
1 T. dry white wine
2 T. orange juice

2 tsp. cornstarch
Fresh raspberries for garnish
   (opt.)

Place thawed raspberries in a blender or food processor and blend until smooth. Sieve, discarding seeds. In a saucepan, combine wine, orange juice, and cornstarch. Add sieved raspberries. Cook and stir until thickened and bubbly. Serve sauce with turkey. Garnish with fresh raspberries, if desired. This sauce also makes a great dessert topping.

Time: 12 minutes under the broiler
Servings: 4

Gloria J. Thompson   *Shiprock*

Gloria is with the Exceptional Programs office of Central Consolidated Schools in Shiprock, New Mexico.

❖

Maggie on Fertilizing
Let's talk dirty...fertilizer. Chicken manure and garden compost work best at Maggie's, plus, they have plenty of it. The original patch was started in a former horse corral with continued contributions from the neighbor's barns and corrals. Yes, you'll have more weeds, but you'll have more berries.

Duck, Orange and Raspberry Salad with Pecans

2 duck legs & thighs, trimmed
2 tsp. fresh lemon juice
1 tsp. minced, fresh tarragon; or 1/4 tsp. dried, crumbled
1 tsp. minced, fresh parsley
Salt & freshly ground black pepper
1/4 c. minced green onions (about 3)
3 T. olive oil

1 1/2 T. fresh lemon juice
Grated peel of 1 orange
1 T. raspberry vinegar (opt.)
1 T. butter
1 garlic clove, unpeeled
1/4 c. coarsely chopped pecans
1 med. orange, peeled thinly, sliced & seeded
Lettuce leaves

Arrange duck in a shallow pan. Combine 2 teaspoons lemon juice with tarragon, parsley, salt, and pepper in a small bowl. Brush over duck. Let stand at room temperature 1 hour.

Preheat broiler. Place duck in broiling pan and broil until browned and crisp, turning once, about 15 minutes per side. Let cool completely.

Cut meat into strips; discard bones (or use in stock). Combine duck and onion in a medium bowl. Whisk olive oil with remaining lemon juice, orange peel, 1 tablespoon raspberry vinegar, and salt and pepper to taste in a small bowl. Pour over duck. Refrigerate at least 2 hours, stirring occasionally.

Meanwhile, melt butter in a small skillet. Add garlic and cook over low heat 1 to 2 minutes. Discard garlic. Add pecans to skillet and cook until browned and crisp, stirring frequently. Remove from heat and set aside.

When ready to serve, add orange slices to duck and toss well. Taste and adjust seasonings. Arrange lettuce leaves on plates and spoon salad over. Sprinkle with pecans and raspberries, and serve.

Joy Jeffrey   *Albuquerque*

Grilled Duck Breast

SAUCE:

1/2 c. raspberry jelly

1/4 c. orange juice

3 T. Chambord liqueur

Combine all sauce ingredients in saucepan and beat over low heat. When jelly turns to liquid, bring to a simmer.

1 duck breast, cleaned

In a bowl, combine sauce and duck breast. Cover and refrigerate for 45 minutes. Grill duck over coals until done and skin is crisp, about 15 to 20 minutes both sides. Serve with wild rice and vegetables. Drizzle remaining sauce, heated, over duck breast.

Jennifer Turner   *Cincinnati, OH*

♥Cornish Game Hens with Mint and Raspberries

4 Cornish game hens

1 (10 oz.) box frozen raspberries

1/2 c. chopped mint

1/4 c. olive oil

2 c. chicken broth

1/2 c. white wine

1 tsp. ground black pepper

Cut Cornish game hens in half lengthwise. Place in bowl. Mix together all remaining ingredients and marinate in refrigerator at least 8 hours, turning hens at least once. Lay hens in a shallow pan and bake at 350° for 25 to 30 minutes, reserving marinade liquid. While hens are baking, boil down marinade to about 1 cup of volume. Remove mint.

Put hen on charcoal grill for about 10 minutes, turning often. Place on platter and pour over reduced marinade. Garnish with fresh mint and fresh raspberries.

Servings: 6

Hens do not have to be put on charcoal grill but they are much better. Do not add salt, because boiled-down broth has plenty. Juice from hens baking in oven can also be added to marinade and boiled down a bit more.

Andrea Fisher   *Santa Fe*

Grilled Pork Tenderloin in Raspberry-Herb Marinade

2 pork tenderloins (each
   about 3/4 lb.; 1 1/2 lb. total)
Raspberry-Herb Marinade
   (recipe follows)

6 T. olive oil
8 to 10 c. washed, crisp, bite-
   size mixed salad greens

Trim and discard surface fat and silvery membrane from pork. Set meat aside. Pour 1/2 cup marinade into a heavy plastic bag. Add tenderloins; seal bag and rotate to coat meat with marinade. Set bag in a pan and chill 2 hours or overnight. Turn bag over occasionally. Add oil to remaining marinade; mix well. Cover and set aside until ready to use. (For a great flavor in the salad, marinate pieces of jicama in some of the remaining marinade mixture.)

Lift meat from marinade. Place tenderloins in center of grill (or broiler). Cover, cook, and baste often. Cook 20 or 30 minutes (meat thermometer should register 155°). Meanwhile, mix reserved marinade and jicama with salad greens. Thinly slice meat across grain. Serve pork with salad, adding salt to taste.

Servings: 4 to 6

RASPBERRY-HERB MARINADE:

1/2 c. raspberry vinegar
2 cloves garlic, minced or
   pressed
1 T. Dijon mustard
1 T. honey
1 tsp. fresh or 1/4 tsp. dried
   marjoram

1 tsp. fresh or 1/4 tsp. dried
   sage
1 tsp. fresh or 1/4 tsp. dried
   thyme
1/2 tsp. coarsely ground
   pepper

Rose Ann Porter   *Albuquerque*

Rose Ann has been very active on the Carrie Tingley Hospital Advisory Board and as a volunteer at the Raspberry Festival. She is the former director of development for the N.M. Museum of Natural History.

♥Berried Pork Salad

1 1/2 c. raspberries
1 1/2 c. blueberries
1 c. strawberries
1 to 1 1/2 lb. boneless pork
tenderloin, thinly sliced into
bite-size pieces

Red leaf lettuce
1 c. chopped green cabbage
Toasted almonds or
macadamia nuts to garnish

Clean and prepare fruit, and set aside. Halve strawberries. Cook pork slices in a pan coated with vegetable spray. Stir-fry until slightly pink. Add cabbage and stir-fry until warm. (Do not overcook.) May be served cold or slightly warm.

To serve, arrange lettuce, fruit, and pork mixture on each plate and pass dressing. Top with nuts. If dressing is prepared ahead, bring to room temperature before serving.

DRESSING:
1/3 c. orange juice
2 T. raspberry vinegar or red
wine vinegar
1 T. raspberry preserves or
fruit spread

1/2 tsp. Dijon mustard
1 T. canola or safflower oil
1 tsp. poppy seeds
1 tsp. finely chopped onion

Combine all ingredients in a jar. Shake well before using.

Servings: 4

Pam Darnell   *Prairie Village, KS*

Raspberry Nutritional Tips
1 c. fresh raspberries = 61 calories; 1.1 grams protein; 3.69 grams fiber; 160 IU Vitamin A; 1.1 grams niacin; 31 mg. Vitamin C; 27 mg. calcium; 22 mg. magnesium; 187 mg. potassium; 0 mg. sodium; .57 mg. zinc; less than 1 gram of fat, 2/3 of which is unsaturated.

♥Papaya and Raspberry Shrimp Salad with Lime Dressing

DRESSING:

1 T. grated fresh lime peel
6 T. freshly squeezed lime
  juice (3 limes)
1 T. honey
3/4 tsp. grated, fresh ginger
  root, or 1/2 tsp. ground
  ginger

1/8 tsp. salt
1/8 tsp. black pepper,
  coarsely ground
3/4 c. vegetable oil

Whisk all dressing ingredients except oil in small bowl. Gradually whisk in oil until blended.

SALAD:

1 ripe papaya (1 1/2 lb.),
  halved lengthwise, seeds
  removed, peeled, cut
  crosswise into 1/4-inch
  thick slices
1 lb. tiny shrimp, cooked &
  shelled (thawed if frozen)

1 1/2 T. grated fresh lime
  peel
Freshly ground pepper
  to taste
1 pt. fresh raspberries
2 thin lime wedges

Put papaya, shrimp, and lime peel in a large bowl. Add 1/3 cup, or just enough dressing to moisten. Toss gently. Mound on serving platter. Grind pepper over top and sprinkle raspberries over all. Garnish platter with lime wedges. Serve remaining dressing separately.

Joy Jeffrey   *Albuquerque*

Big Bay Salad en Baguette

VINAIGRETTE:

2 T. Salman Ranch Raspberry
Vinegar

2 T. extra virgin olive oil
1 tsp. walnut oil

Whisk all ingredients together.

SALAD:

1 (6 oz.) can water-packed light
tuna, drained
1/3 c. green pepper, chopped
1/3 c. red bell pepper, chopped
1/2 c. pineapple chunks
1/3 c. cashew pieces
3 scallions, chopped

1 sm. celery rib, chopped
1/2 tsp. fresh ginger root,
minced
Freshly ground pepper to
taste
1 baguette, cut in half
crosswise

Preheat oven to 350°. Mix salad and season with pepper. Toss with well-whisked vinaigrette. Hollow out baguette and fill with salad. Place on cookie sheet. Bake 15 minutes, or until baguette is crisp. Cut into 1-inch slices and serve as canapes or luncheon sandwiches.

Time: 15 minutes
Temperature: 350°
Servings: 8 to 10

Salman Family   *La Cueva*

Storing Raspberries
Depending on the weather, humidity, temperature, and the ripeness of the berries you pick, raspberries will keep under refrigeration for one to six days.

Vegetables

Beets with Raspberry Vinegar and Anise

4 to 5 fresh beets, cooked (or one 16 oz. canned, drained, whole, sliced or julienned beets)

1/2 sm. red or white onion, chopped

Peel fresh, cooked beets and cut into 3/4-inch slices. Cut each slice into four "sticks". (Use julienne beets for smaller slices for a side dish.) Add onion and mix with beets.

DRESSING:
6 T. extra virgin olive oil
3 T. raspberry vinegar

Dash of salt & pepper
1 T. crushed anise seeds

Beat ingredients together in a medium-size bowl. Add to beets and onions; toss. Cover and refrigerate several hours, or up to a day to let flavors blend. Serve at room temperature.

Servings: 4 to 6

Marianne Dickinson   *Albuquerque*

Marianne is a writer and neighborhood activist. She is the production coordinator of the Very Special Raspberry Cookbook.

Carrot Salad with Raspberry Vinaigrette

2/3 c. fresh parsley leaves, chopped
1/3 c. vegetable oil (preferably olive)
3 T. raspberry vinegar
2 tsp. Dijon mustard

1 tsp. sugar
1/2 tsp. cinnamon
1/2 tsp. salt
Freshly ground pepper
2 lb. carrots, shredded

Reserve 2 tablespoons chopped parsley. Shake all ingredients, except carrots, together in a covered jar. Add mixture to carrots; cover and refrigerate. Just before serving, garnish with reserved parsley.

Servings: 8

Joy Jeffrey   *Albuquerque*

Carrots with Raspberry Marinade

1 1/2 lb. carrots
Boiling water, with salt added
1/3 c. raspberry vinegar

1 tsp. salt (optional)
1/2 tsp. freshly ground
   pepper
1/2 c. extra-virgin olive oil

Peel the carrots and cut slices 1/8-inch thick. Add them to salted, boiling water. Cook them until nearly tender, about 5 minutes. They should still be slightly crunchy. Drain. Put them in a medium-sized bowl and sprinkle with raspberry vinegar, salt, and pepper. Do this while the carrots are still hot. Add enough oil to cover the carrots, and toss well. Refrigerate 3 to 4 hours, or overnight. They will keep for several days. Serve at room temperature. Lift them from their marinade and add more seasonings if necessary.

This is a flavor mixture of sweet and spicy. It is delicious as part of an antipasto or side dish with chicken or pork. An addition of diced bell peppers and green onions adds extra flavor.

Mary Blank   *Albuquerque*

Sweet Potatoes
with Raspberries

8 med. sweet potatoes
1 tsp. salt
1/4 c. firmly packed brown
   sugar

1/4 c. butter or margarine,
   softened
1 (10 oz) pkg. frozen
   raspberries, thawed

Cook sweet potatoes in boiling, salted water 20 to 25 minutes, or until tender. Drain, cool, peel, and cut lengthwise. Arrange potatoes in a lightly greased 9x13x2-inch casserole, cut-side up. Combine brown sugar and butter in a small bowl; mix well. Spread brown sugar mixture over cut surface of potatoes. Top with raspberries and their juice.

Bake, uncovered, at 350° for 25 minutes, spooning raspberries and juice from pan over potatoes occasionally.

Time: 25 minutes
Temperature: 350°
Servings: 8 to 10

Judith R. Harris   *Albuquerque*

"Three Little Pigs"
Skye Steed - Age 6
Nob Hill Elementary, Ruidoso
"Start With the Arts" residency program

Desserts

Raspberry Pizza

CRUST:
1 c. flour

1 stick butter or margarine
1/2 c. powdered sugar

Blend and knead into dough. Spread on pizza pan and bake 10 minutes at 350°.

FILLING:
8 oz. cream cheese
1 can condensed milk

1 tsp. vanilla
1/3 c. lemon juice
1 pt. fresh raspberries

Combine cream cheese, milk, vanilla, and lemon juice. Spread over cooled crust. Top with raspberries and cover with raspberry glaze.

GLAZE:
1 c. raspberries
1 c. sugar

1 c. water
2 1/2 T. cornstarch

In a saucepan, combine raspberries, 3/4 cup sugar, and water. Cook until berries are soft. Add 1/4 cup sugar mixed with 2 1/2 tablespoons cornstarch. Cook until thick and glazed.

The Honorable Joe Skeen   *Washington, D.C.*

Joe Skeen represents the 2nd district of New Mexico in the United States House of Representatives.
    "Please find enclosed a copy of a recipe with raspberries that I find most enjoyable. Enjoy!!"

"Chile Kissed Ya."

LEMON CURD:
2 eggs
Grated peel of 1 lemon

1/3 c. fresh lemon juice (1 to 2 lemons)
1/3 c. granulated sugar
4 T. butter, cut into pieces

Whisk eggs in small bowl and set aside. Heat the remaining ingredients over medium heat. Gradually pour hot liquid over the eggs, whisking continuously. Return the mixture to the saucepan and whisk over medium heat until thick and beginning to simmer. Strain into a clean container to cool. (Can be made up to a week in advance; keep refrigerated.)

JALAPEÑO-RASPBERRY SAUCE:
2 c. fresh or 12 oz. frozen
  raspberries, thawed (optional:
  strain to remove seeds for
  smoother sauce)
2 T. orange-flavored liqueur or
  orange juice

1 to 2 tsp. (or more) minced,
  bottled jalapeño chiles
2 to 3 tsp. liquid from
  jalapeño bottle

Process all ingredients in blender until smooth. (Also can be refrigerated up to a week, but it will get hotter!)

CHILE AND STUFFING:
8 oz. cream cheese, warmed
  to room temperature
1 T. sugar
1/2 tsp. vanilla
1/4 c. chopped piñon or
  pistachio nuts

8 sprigs fresh mint (optional)
8 fresh green chiles, roasted,
  peeled & seeded; or 2
  (7 oz.) cans whole chiles,
  drained & patted dry

To assemble: blend cream cheese, sugar, and vanilla in medium-size bowl with electric mixer until smooth. Fold in the lemon curd. (Don't overblend.) Stuff 2 tablespoons cream cheese mixture into each green chile. Turn rellenos onto individual serving plates. Spoon 1 to 2 tablespoons raspberry sauce over each chile and sprinkle with chopped nuts. Garnish with sprigs of mint if desired. Serve more raspberry sauce as desired.

Servings: 8

Continued on following page.

Continued from preceding page.

Bill Balassi, Robin Casaus   *Albuquerque*

Robin and Bill are friends who get together with several other guitarists on Wednesday nights. One night, after playing the Everly Brothers' "Till I Kissed Ya", Bill suggested that there ought to be a dessert named "Chile Kissed Ya". Robin agreed, and together they developed the recipe you see here. It debuted to rave reviews at the 1992 Raspberry Festival.

Fontaine au Chocolat Et Framboises

7 oz. bittersweet chocolate,
   chopped
1/2 c. cream
1/2 c. sugar
1/3 c. boiling water
4 oz. unsalted butter, melted
8 sheets filo dough

3 T. granulated sugar
12 (2 1/2-inch) rounds of plain
   chocolate cake, 1/2-inch
   thick
1 pt. raspberries
1 c. heavy cream, whipped
Mint sprigs

Place chopped chocolate in small bowl. Heat cream to boiling, pour over chocolate. Stir until chocolate is completely melted and smooth. Set aside to cool; do not refrigerate.

Dissolve sugar in boiling water; set aside. Spread 1 sheet of filo dough on work surface. Brush with butter and sprinkle with 1 teaspoon sugar. Cut the filo into three 5-inch-wide strips. Place a round of cake in the center of each strip. Brush with the sugar-water mixture, then top with a generous spoonful of the chocolate mixture. Top the chocolate with 8 to 10 berries. Fold 1 end of the filo over the top, tucking it under the cake. Fold the other end over; tuck in the sides and fold under to make a little package, enclosing the filling completely. Brush with butter and sprinkle with sugar. Repeat until filo dough and cake are all used.

Place on buttered tray. Refrigerate until ready to bake. Heat oven to 350°. Bake pastries 15 minutes or until lightly browned. Let stand 5 minutes. Serve garnished with whipped cream and mint sprigs.

Time: 15 minutes
Temperature: 350°
Servings: 12

Rosalind Simpson   *Santa Fe*

Rosalind is a classical musician participating in Very Special Arts New Mexico's Artist in Residence programs.

Chocolate Truffle Loaf with Raspberry Sauce

1/2 c. heavy cream	1/2 c. margarine
3 egg yolks	1 1/2 c. heavy cream
16 (1 oz.) sq. semisweet	1/4 c. confectioners' sugar
chocolate	1 tsp. sugar
1/2 c. light or dark corn syrup	

Line a 9 1/4 x 5 1/4 x 2 3/4-inch loaf pan with plastic wrap. In small bowl, mix 1/2 cup cream with the egg yolks. In large saucepan, combine chocolate, corn syrup, and margarine; stir over medium heat until melted. Add egg mixture. Cook 3 minutes over medium heat, stirring constantly.* Cool to room temperature.

In small bowl, with mixer at medium speed, beat 1 1/2 cups cream, sugar, and vanilla until soft peaks form. Gently fold into chocolate mixture just until combined. Pour into prepared pan. Cover with plastic wrap. Refrigerate overnight or chill in freezer 3 hours. Slice and serve with raspberry sauce. Garnish with chocolate leaves and fresh berries.

*Microwave can be used to this point: Prepare the pan and egg mixture as above. In a 3-quart microwavable bowl, mix chocolate, corn syrup, and margarine. Microwave on HIGH (100%) 2 to 2 1/2 minutes or until melted, stirring twice. Stir in egg mixture. Microwave 3 minutes, stirring twice.

RASPBERRY SAUCE:

1 (10 oz.) pkg. raspberries,	1/3 c. light corn syrup
thawed	

In blender or food processor, purée raspberries; strain to remove seeds. Stir in 1/3 cup light corn syrup; blend.

Servings: 12

Deborah Marie McElligott   *Mesilla*

Microwave Raspberry Buckle

3/4 c. sugar
1/4 c. margarine, room
    temperature
1 egg
1/2 c. milk

1 1/2 c. flour
2 tsp. baking powder
1/2 tsp. salt
2 c. fresh or thawed frozen
    raspberries

Beat sugar, margarine, and egg until fluffy. Blend in milk. Combine dry ingredients and add to egg mixture, mixing thoroughly. Fold in raspberries. Line an 8x8- or 9x9-inch glass or microwave-safe dish with 2 thicknesses of paper towels. Spread batter evenly in baking dish.

TOPPING:
1/2 c. brown sugar
1/3 c. flour
1/2 tsp. cinnamon

1/4 c. butter or margarine,
    room temperature

Combine brown sugar, flour, and cinnamon. Cut in butter until mixture is crumbly; sprinkle over batter. Tap dish on counter to let the air bubbles escape, and let stand 10 minutes. Cook 4 minutes on medium-high; rotate 1/4. Cook 4 more minutes; turn. Cook 3 more minutes and check for doneness; top will still be very moist. If microwave has a broiling element, broil for 1 minute or until lightly browned. You may broil this in a conventional broiler for 3 minutes.

Allow to cool slightly and serve. The whole cake can be inverted onto a serving tray and topped with whipped cream or ice cream.

Time: 9 to 12 minutes
Temperature: Medium-high in microwave
Servings: 8 to 10 minutes

John Baggerly   *Albuquerque*

John is an ex-officio member of the Board of Directors of Very Special Arts New Mexico. He has contributed countless hours as an artist and as an administrator.

Raspberry Chocolate Terrine

RASPBERRY PURÉE:

1 1/2 pt. raspberries
1/2 c. sugar

1/2 c. water

Purée raspberries in blender or food processor. Strain out seeds through fine strainer or cheesecloth. Make simple syrup with sugar and water by boiling 2 minutes. Stir into raspberries and refrigerate.

CHOCOLATE TERRINE:

14 oz. semisweet chocolate
1/4 lb. butter

2 eggs
1 1/2 c. heavy cream, whipped

Melt chocolate and butter in double boiler. Pour into a large bowl and set aside. Beat eggs lightly and pour into double boiler. Be sure water is boiling. Take about 4 minutes to thicken eggs, whisking constantly. Whip cream until slightly thickened. Blend eggs into chocolate mixture. Fold whipped cream into chocolate mixture. Line mold (loaf pan 8 1/2 x 4 1/2 x 2 1/2-inches) with plastic wrap. Turn half of mixture into mold pan. Add layer of Macaroon Chambord.

MACAROON CHAMBORD:

4 oz. almond flour (skinless,
   toasted ground almonds)
1 egg white

1/4 c. sugar
2 T. Chambord (raspberry
   liqueur)

Preheat oven to 350°. Mix almond flour, egg white, and sugar into a paste. (Can substitute almond macaroons and soak in Chambord for 5 minutes.) Put mixture 1 inch thick on cookie sheet. Bake at 350° for 12 minutes or until golden brown. Sprinkle with Chambord while still warm. Cut macaroon to fit mold, leaving a 1/2-inch chocolate border. Put macaroon in mold and add rest of chocolate mixture. Refrigerate 4 hours or more.

To serve, pour thin layer of raspberry purée on dessert plates. Slice terrine. Put 1 slice on each plate. Garnish with fresh raspberries and mint. Whipped cream is optional.

Time: 12 minutes
Temperature: 35°
Servings: 8 to 10

Continued on following page.

Continued from preceding page.

This dessert will keep well in the refrigerator for 10 days, the freezer for up to 6 weeks.

Jane and Daniel Blumenfeld   *Albuquerque*

Jane is a very active member of the Raspberry Festival Committee. She and her son Daniel created this recipe.

Raspberry Crepes

FILLING:

10 oz. frozen raspberries,   1/3 c. sauterne wine
   thawed   1 T. butter
1 1/2 T. cornstarch

Combine berries, cornstarch, and wine in a heavy saucepan. Add butter and cook until thickened, stirring constantly. Set aside.

CREPES: 1/4 c. flour, sifted
6 eggs   3 T. confectioners' sugar
1/4 tsp. salt   Oil for brushing pan (canola
2 T. water   or corn work best)

In blender, combine eggs, salt, water, flour, and sugar. Using crepe pan or a small Teflon-coated pan, brush with oil after heating to moderate-high heat. Pour in about 2 to 3 tablespoons batter, tilting from side to side into a thin layer. Using a knife or spatula, lift crepe when edges look dry and turn over to cook only a few seconds. Lay on oiled wax paper. Store until needed, in refrigerator, covered with foil. Crepes can be frozen.

To serve, separate crepes and reheat in 275° oven. Reheat sauce. Spoon about 2 tablespoons of warm sauce on a crepe; roll up. Repeat with remaining crepes and place on an ovenproof platter. Pour remaining sauce over the crepes and keep warm in the oven. Dust with powdered sugar just before serving.

Yields 10 crepes

Robert Migneault   *Albuquerque*

Robert Migneault is the Dean of the University of New Mexico Libraries.

Flaming Pears Melba

2 lg. (1 lb. 13 oz.) cans pear
   halves

Drain pears, reserving syrup. Place pear halves, cut side down, on paper toweling.

FILLING:

1 (3 oz.) pkg. cream cheese,   1/4 c. chopped walnuts
   softened

Combine cream cheese, sugar, and enough pear syrup to make mix of spreading consistency. Stir in walnuts. Spread cream cheese mixture in hollow of each pear, using about 1 tablespoon for each. Press 2 halves together making 6 pears.

SAUCE: 1 (10 oz.) pkg. frozen rasp-
1 T. cornstarch   berries, thawed
1/4 c. water   1/4 c. brandy

In saucepan, blend water and cornstarch. Stir in raspberries. Cook and stir until thickened. Press through a sieve. In small pan, preheat brandy.* Pour brandy on top of raspberry sauce and ignite at table with long match. Immediately spoon flaming sauce over pears and enjoy.

*Care must be taken not to get it too hot. The first time Lili made a flaming dish, it was on a gas range. It ignited as she was removing it from the flame. Startled, she jerked her hand and pan, sending flames everywhere, burning her tiny hostess apron, leaving only the tie string. If this should happen, keep your cool and smother the fire with a lid.

Servings: 6 to 10

Lili Del Costillo   *Albuquerque*

Lili Del Costello is a Flamenco dancer, well-known throughout New Mexico for her choreography and stunning performances. She is one of the prominent Hispanic women featured in the book Nuestras Mujeres...Hispanas of New Mexico.

♥Pears Poached in Sauterne with Raspberry Sauce

4 to 6 ripe Bosc pears	1/2 cinnamon stick
1 bottle sauterne	Mint sprigs for garnish
1/3 c. sugar	

Peel and core pears, leaving stems attached. Slice a small piece off the bottom of each pear to leave a flat base. Rub pears with lemon juice. Bring sauterne to a boil in a heavy saucepan and add sugar and cinnamon stick. Reduce heat to simmer and poach pears in sauterne 30 to 40 minutes until tender. Remove pears from poaching liquid. Drain, and refrigerate.

RASPBERRY SAUCE:

1 basket raspberries (reserve a few for garnish)	2 T. Framboise (raspberry liqueur)
Confectioners' sugar, to taste	

Purée raspberries and pass through sieve to remove seeds. Sweeten with sugar and add Framboise.

To serve, place a pear upright on a dessert plate and spoon raspberry sauce around the pear. Garnish with mint sprigs and a few of the reserved raspberries.

Servings: 4 to 6

Robert W. Jahnke, MD   *Albuquerque*

Robert Jahnke, M.D., is chief of Neuroradiology at Albuquerque's Lovelace Medical Center and Clinical Associate Professor of Radiology at the University of New Mexico and at Stanford University School of Medicine. Cooking is his "main avocation, self-taught, learned through cookbooks."

Raspberry Dumplings

2 c. all-purpose flour
4 tsp. baking powder
1 T. sugar
3/4 tsp. salt
1/3 c. shortening
1 beaten egg
1/2 c. milk

1 c. fresh or frozen, lightly
   sweetened raspberries,
   thawed
1/3 c. sugar
1/4 tsp. ground cinnamon
Lemon Sauce

Stir together flour, baking powder, 1 tablespoon sugar, and salt. Cut in shortening until mixture resembles coarse crumbs. Combine egg and milk. Stir into flour mixture. Turn out onto lightly floured surface. Gently knead 8 to 10 strokes. Roll out into a 15x10-inch rectangle. Cut into six 5x5-inch squares. Spoon berries onto squares. Combine 1/3 cup sugar and cinnamon. Sprinkle over berries. Moisten edges of each square. Fold corners of each square to center over berries; seal edges. Place on foil-lined baking sheet. Bake in 400° oven for 15 to 20 minutes. Serve warm with Lemon Sauce.

LEMON SAUCE:
3 T. sugar
2 tsp. cornstarch
1/2 c. cold water
1/2 tsp. finely shredded
   lemon peel

1 T. lemon juice
1/2 c. frozen whipped dessert
   topping, thawed

Combine sugar and cornstarch. Stir in water. Cook and stir until bubbly. Stir in lemon peel and juice; cool. Fold in thawed dessert topping.

Time: 15 to 20 minutes
Temperature: 400°
Servings: 6

Joy Jeffrey   *Albuquerque*

Shopping for Raspberries
When selecting fresh berries, look for clean, bright, plump berries with a uniform
color. Avoid berries with caps underripe, and dirty, mashed, moldy or wet berries.
Remember one pint serves three people.

Rødgrød

1 1/2 lb. fresh raspberries or
    1 (10 oz.) pkg. frozen berries
    (fresh strawberries may
    substitute for half the
    berries)
2 T. sugar

2 T. arrowroot
1/4 c. cold water
Toasted slivered almonds
Cream, half & half, whipped
    or dessert topping

Wash fresh berries or defrost frozen ones. Place raspberries and sugar in blender, and process a few minutes until smooth. Transfer to heavy 1 1/2-quart stainless steel pan. Bring to a boil while stirring. Quickly mix the arrowroot and water. Add to berries, letting mixture return to simmer, but NOT boiling, until thickened. Remove from heat and pour into individual servers. If using crystal or fine china, allow to cool 30 minutes. Decorate with almonds just before serving and pass cream of choice. The Danes usually use half & half or nothing.

Rodgrod is a Danish national dessert. It is wonderful after meat or game!

Servings: 6 (doubles easily)

Janet Matwiyoff   *Albuquerque*

Thawing Raspberries
A method that should help berries retain their shape when thawed is to freeze them in a sugar syrup (1 cup sugar dissolved in 3 cups boiling water, then cooled). Fill a rigid container with berries, cover with syrup, leaving 1/2-inch on top for expansion. When thawing individually frozen berries, use the microwave, one minute at medium, on a paper towel.

♥Lowfat Natillas

3 eggs or egg substitutes	3 egg whites
1/4 c. flour	Nutmeg
4 c. skim milk	Cinnamon
3/4 c. sugar	Fresh raspberries
1/4 tsp. salt	

Place eggs or egg substitute, flour, and a cup of skim milk in a small mixing bowl. Stir to make a smooth paste; set aside. Place the remaining milk, sugar, and salt in a heavy medium-size saucepan and scald at medium heat. Add the egg mixture to the scalded milk and continue to cook at medium heat until a soft custard consistency is reached. Remove custard from heat and allow to cool at room temperature.

Beat the egg whites in a medium-size mixing bowl until they are stiff, but not dry. Fold the egg whites into the custard. Serve warm or cool. Garnish with nutmeg, cinnamon and fresh raspberries before serving.

Loretta Armenta   *Albuquerque*

Loretta is a member of the Carrie Tingley Advisory Board and the Foundation Board. She has enjoyed creating lowfat Mexican food recipes for her family. She is also Special Projects Director for the Hispano Chamber of Commerce.

♥Raspberry Crème Brûlee

2 c. nonfat milk	1/3 c. + 2 T. sugar
2 T. nonfat milk powder	1 tsp. vanilla
3/4 c. thawed frozen egg substitute	30 fresh raspberries

Stir together 1/2 cup nonfat milk and nonfat milk powder until blended. Stir in remaining nonfat milk, egg substitute, 1/2 cup sugar, and vanilla. Place 5 raspberries in bottom of each of six 5-ounce custard cups. Pour custard mixture into cups. Place custard cups in a pan filled with hot water just 1 inch in depth and bake at 325°, about 35 minutes, or until custard is set; chill. Sprinkle 1/2 teaspoon sugar over top of each custard and place on baking sheets. Broil 4 inches from heat until sugar is caramelized.

Time: 35 minutes
Temperature: 325°
Servings: 6

Beth Rosenstein   *Albuquerque*

♥ Finnish Fruit Pudding

PUDDING:

3 c. orange juice
1/3 c. honey
Juice of 1/2 lemon
1/2 c. non-instant cream of
  wheat

1 c. fresh or unsweetened
  frozen raspberries
Dash of cinnamon & nutmeg
1 c. nonfat yogurt

Bring juices and honey to a boil. Sprinkle in cream of wheat and cook slowly, stirring, until thick and smooth (8 minutes). Remove from heat. Whip 15 minutes in stationary (if available) electric mixer until light and fluffy. (Let the mixer go while you make the sauce.) Fold in berries, spices, and yogurt. Chill in a 2-quart casserole or glass bowl for 1 1/2 hours.

SAUCE:

1 c. raspberries
2 T. sugar

1/4 c. water

Combine berries, sugar, and water in blender. Spoon over pudding to serve.

This absolutely delicious and much requested dessert is 100% nonfat and very low sugar.

Servings: 4 to 6

Joan Weissman

Joan Weissman is an artist who works in ceramics. She works with Seniors and has been active throughout Albuquerque's "1% for Art" program.

Raspberry Custard

3/4 c. granulated sugar
1/3 c. all-purpose flour
Dash of salt
4 egg yolks

2 c. milk
1/2 tsp. vanilla extract
1 c. raspberries

Combine sugar, flour and salt in top of double boiler. Stir in 4 egg yolks and milk; blend well. Cook, uncovered, over boiling water, stirring constantly until thickened. Reduce heat and cook, stirring occasionally, for 5 minutes. Remove from heat; add vanilla. Pour custard into oblong dish or individual serving dishes; let cool. Refrigerate until firm. Serve with raspberry garnish.

Servings: 6 to 10

Lorena T. Sanchez   *Las Vegas*

Lorena Sanchez is from Las Vegas, New Mexico. Her husband, Gilbert, was president of Highlands University there. Lorena is an accomplished artist whose watercolors are sold state-wide.

Raspberry Rice Surprise

1 c. uncooked rice
3 c. boiling water
3/4 tsp. salt
1/2 c. sugar

2 T. honey
1/4 tsp. almond extract
1 c. heavy cream, whipped

Cook rice in boiling water with salt added, until tender and fluffy. (Liquid should be absorbed by rice.) Blend in 1/2 cup sugar, honey, and almond extract. Chill. Fold in whipped cream.

SAUCE:
1 T. cornstarch
1/2 c. sugar
1/4 c. cold water

2 c. red raspberries
1 T. lemon juice

In a saucepan, mix cornstarch and 1/2 cup sugar. Add cold water and stir until smooth. Add raspberries and lemon juice. Bring to a boil; reduce heat and simmer 5 minutes. Chill. Top each serving of rice with raspberry sauce.

Servings: 6

Deborah Marie McElligott   *Mesilla*

Zabaglione

5 egg yolks + 1 whole egg (can use 2 c. egg substitute)	1/2 c. Marsala, cream sherry, or Madeira wine
6 T. granulated sugar	1 to 2 pt. fresh raspberries

Beat eggs and sugar well. Add wine gradually in a steel mixing bowl. Place over boiling water or in a double boiler and whisk constantly as custard thickens. Remove from heat and whisk another minute or two, Pour custard into berry-filled glasses, or chill and serve as an accompaniment to berries.

Servings: 6 to 8

Mary Blank   *Albuquerque*

Pavlova

4 egg whites at room temperature	2 tsp. white wine vinegar
1/4 tsp. salt	1 tsp. vanilla extract
1/4 tsp. cream of tartar	1 c. heavy cream, whipped
1 c. fine granulated sugar	2 to 3 c. raspberries, sliced & sprinkled with sugar &
4 tsp. cornstarch	Grand Marnier

Preheat oven to 275°.

Beat egg whites, salt, and cream of tartar together in a bowl until the whites hold a stiff peak. Add the sugar, a few tablespoons at a time, beating until mixture is stiff and glossy. Beat in cornstarch, then vinegar and vanilla. Butter and lightly flour an 8-inch pan with a removable bottom. Fill gently with mixture, spreading it higher around the edges than in the center to form a depression. Bake for 1 to 1 1/4 hours or until slightly browned. Cool slightly. Unmold and slide onto serving plate. Let cool completely. Just before serving, spread with whipped cream and then with raspberries.

Time: 1 to 1 1/4 hours
Temperature: 275°
Servings: 4 to 6

Beverly Forman   *Albuquerque*

Beverly Forman is the Development Director of the Kidney Foundation of New Mexico.

♥Denim and Lace

Denim trousers & jacket
1 oz. Chambord liqueur
2 oz. chocolate chips

1 insulated cup
1 c. raspberries

Dress in the denim trousers and jacket. Place liqueur and chips in an insulated container (insulated cup inside an aluminum one serves well) and take them on a hike up a small, high canyon where you know there is a wild patch of raspberries. Once at the raspberry patch, collect about 1 cup worth of raspberries. Eat the plumpest, most perfect just as they are, taking care not to overeat; you'll just have to pick more if you do! Place the second half of the raspberries in cup with the chocolate chips. Sit in a comfortable spot with a view, pour the Chambord over them and brace yourself! It's a treat for all the senses.

Servings: 1

Luis Campos   *Albuquerque*

Luis Campos is a guitarist who has worked with Very Special Arts New Mexico. His passion for the guitar led him to start guitar lessons at the age of 10. His first commercially produced tape is titled Torre.

Fruit Desserts

Banana-Raspberry Flambé

3 T. butter or margarine
1 T. brown sugar
6 med. bananas, sliced

1 (10 oz.) pkg. frozen raspberries, thawed
6 T. orange liqueur
2 T. granulated sugar

Melt butter. Add brown sugar until dissolved. Add banana and cook 2 to 3 minutes over medium heat. Combine raspberries, 2 tablespoons liqueur, and granulated sugar in blender until smooth. Add to bananas; heat through. Heat remaining liqueur in ladle or small pan. Flame and pour over fruit. Serve over ice cream.

Servings: 4 cups

Carmela Bentz   *Las Cruces*

♥Fresh Pineapple with Raspberry Sauce

1 (12 oz.) pkg. frozen
  unsweetened raspberries,
  thawed
2 T. powdered sugar, sifted
1 T. cherry-flavored brandy
  (optional)

2 fresh ripe pineapples,
  peeled, sliced into 3/4-inch
  rings, well chilled
Mint leaves (optional)

In food processor or blender, purée raspberries until smooth. Place fine mesh sieve over bowl and press purée through sieve; discard seeds. Stir in sugar. Stir in brandy (optional). Arrange 2 pineapple rings on each individual dessert plate and spoon portion of sauce on top. Garnish with mint leaves, if desired. Pass remaining sauce separately.

Servings: 8 to 12

Art Ortiz, Santa Fe Chili, Inc. *Santa Fe*

Raspberry-Fruit Fondue

RASPBERRY DIP:
1/2 pt. fresh raspberries or
  2 (10 oz.) pkg. frozen raspberries, thawed & drained

2 T. sugar
1 (8 oz.) pkg. cream cheese,
  softened

In covered blender container, thoroughly blend raspberries and sugar. Sieve raspberries to remove seeds. In a medium bowl, beat cream cheese until smooth with a mixer at medium speed. Gradually beat in raspberry pulp until smooth. Refrigerate.

FRUITS:
2 pears, cut into thin wedges
Lemon juice
1/2 pt. strawberries

1/2 honeydew melon, scooped
  into balls
1/2 pineapple, cut into strips
Cinnamon

Sprinkle pears with lemon juice; arrange with other fruits on a platter around the bowl of dip. Sprinkle all fruit with cinnamon. Use cocktail forks for dipping.

Servings: 6

Janet Lindsay *Shiprock, NM*

This was contributed for the cookbook by Janet for her class at Tse'Bit'A'i' Middle School in Shiprock, New Mexico.

♥Strawberries with Raspberry Sauce

1 qt. fresh ripe strawberries
1 T. honey

2 1/2 T. fresh lemon juice
10 oz. frozen raspberries

Wash, dry, and hull strawberries. Mix honey and lemon juice. Mix with strawberries. Thaw raspberries and whirl in blender to make a sauce. Serve strawberries topped with sauce.

Servings: 4

Carol Kinney *Albuquerque*

♥Melon and Raspberries in Rum-Lime Sauce

1 cantaloupe
1 sm. honeydew melon
1/8 of a small watermelon
1 c. raspberries

Chopped candied ginger
(optional)
Mint sprigs for garnish

Using a melon scoop, form the melon into balls. Work around the seeds when scooping watermelon balls. Pile melon balls into a serving bowl.

RUM-LIME SAUCE:
2/3 c. sugar
1/3 c. water

1 tsp. lime rind, grated
1/2 c. light rum

In a small saucepan, mix sugar and water. Bring to a boil. Reduce heat and simmer for 5 minutes. Add the lime rind and cool to room temperature. Stir in lime juice and rum. Pour the sauce over the melon balls.

Gently stir in raspberries and add chopped candied ginger if desired. Chill, covered, for several hours. Decorate with sprigs of mint and add additional rum, if desired.

Servings: 4 to 6

Jennie Goff & Lynn Dehler, The Harvest *Albuquerque*

♥Elegant Fruit Salad

1 (10 oz.) pkg. frozen red
  raspberries, thawed
2 oz. creme de cassis
3 sliced bananas
1 pt. blueberries
1 pt. strawberries, hulled

1 c. green grapes (optional)
3 peaches
Any colorful fresh seasonal
  fruit that mixes with the
  above

Purée raspberries in food processor. Add creme de cassis. Prepare and combine fruits. Mix gently with raspberry purée.

Looks gorgeous in a crystal bowl! This could be served as a side dish for brunch or breakfast or served over angel cake or yellow cake with whipped cream or ice cream as a dessert.

Servings: 6 to 8

Dr. Dale and Jennifer Alverson   *Albuquerque*

Dr. Alverson is Director of Neonatology at UNM's Medical School and gives health advice on Albuquerque's NBC-TV affiliate. He was a celebrity chef at the 1991 Raspberry Festival.

❖

Eating Raspberries
It is best to use raspberries as soon as possible. Natural berry sweetness varies with sun and rain, so add sugar to taste. Or use less sugar and add lemon juice which enhances raspberry flavor. Fresh berries taste best at room temperature.

Gelatins & Mousses

Grapefruit Mousse with Crushed Raspberries

3/4 c. frozen grapefruit juice
concentrate (preferably
pink), thawed
3/4 . sugar
Pinch of salt
1 T. fresh lemon juice (optional)

1 env. unflavored gelatin,
softened in 1/4 c. cold
water
1 tsp. grated lemon zest
2 c. heavy cream, whipped
1 pt. raspberries

In a small saucepan, over medium heat, combine grapefruit concentrate, sugar, salt, and lemon juice. Stir in dissolved gelatin and simmer about 3 minutes; whisk in lemon zest. Allow mixture to completely cool and thicken slightly. Fold in whipped cream. Pour mixture into a 1-quart fluted mold. Refrigerate until set, at least 2 hours.

Just before serving, crush raspberries slightly in a small bowl. Taste and add more sugar or lemon juice if desired. Unmold mousse onto a plate and gently pour raspberries on top. Add fresh raspberries around the edge for a beautiful dessert.

Servings: 6

Jean Kennedy Smith   *Washington, D.C.*

Jean Kennedy Smith is the founder of Very Special Arts. At present, Mrs. Smith is the United States Ambassador to Ireland.

Chocolate Mousse
and Raspberries

MOUSSE:

4 (4 oz.) bars unsweetened
   chocolate, broken into
   pieces
1 (14 oz.) can sweetened
   condensed milk

2 tsp. vanilla extract
2 c. cold whipping cream

In heavy saucepan over medium-low heat, melt chocolate with sweetened condensed milk. Stir in vanilla. Pour into large bowl and cool to room temperature, about 1 1/2 hours. Beat until smooth. In large mixing bowl, beat cream until stiff. Fold into chocolate mixture. Spoon mousse into dessert dishes. Refrigerate until thoroughly chilled. Serve with Raspberry Topping.

RASPBERRY TOPPING:

1 (10 oz.) pkg. thawed frozen
   red raspberries

1/4 c. red currant jelly or red
   raspberry jam
1 T. cornstarch

Drain thawed raspberries, reserving syrup. In small saucepan, stir together 2/3 cup reserved syrup, jelly or jam, and cornstarch. Cook over low heat, stirring constantly until thickened and clear. Stir in raspberries.

Servings: 8

William H. Johnson

William Johnson is the CEO of the University of New Mexico Hospital.

Raspberry Gelatin Dessert

CRUST:

1 1/2 c. crushed pretzels   3/4 c. melted butter
2 T. sugar

Press into a 9x13-inch pan. Bake 10 minutes at 350°. Cool.

FILLING:

8 oz. cream cheese   12 oz. frozen whipped topping
1 c. sugar

Fold in and spread over cooled crust.

TOPPING:

2 c. boiling water   2 (10 oz.) pkgs. frozen rasp-
1 (6 oz.) pkg. strawberry or   berries, thawed
   raspberry gelatin

Prepare gelatin according to directions. Add raspberries. Spread over cream cheese mixture. Chill in refrigerator overnight.

Time: 10 minutes
Temperature: 350°
Servings: 12

Peggy Pritchett   *Santa Fe*

Verena's Russian Creme with Fresh Raspberry Topping

1 3/4 c. light cream   1 1/2 c. thick sour cream,
1 c. sugar   whipped
2 T. gelatin   1 tsp. vanilla
1/2 c. cold water   1 pt. fresh raspberries

Heat light cream with sugar until sugar dissolves. Soak gelatin in cold water and combine with the hot cream. Fold in whipped sour cream and vanilla as the mixture begins to congeal. Pour into a ring or individual molds. Serve with fresh or frosted raspberries.

Servings: 6 to 8

Belle K. Conway   *Albuquerque*

Sour Cream Bavarian and Raspberry Sauce

1 env. unflavored gelatin	1 (10 oz.) pkg. frozen
2/3 c. sugar	raspberries
3/4 c. boiling water	Water
1 c. sour cream	1 T. sugar
1 tsp. vanilla	1 T. cornstarch
2 c. thawed, prepared	
nondairy whipped topping	

Combine gelatin and sugar. Add boiling water and stir until dissolved. Blend in sour cream and vanilla. Chill until slightly thickened. Blend in nondairy topping. Pour into buttered 9-ounce mold. Chill until firm—about 3 hours; unmold. Serve with fruit sauce. Makes 1 pint.

Drain thawed raspberries, measuring syrup. Add water to syrup to make 3/4 cup. Blend in 1 tablespoon each sugar and cornstarch. Cook and stir over medium heat until mixture is thickened and clear. Add fruit. Chill. Makes about 1 1/2 cups.

Servings: 6 to 8

Bob Bovinette   *Albuquerque*

Bob Bovinette is Head Master of the Albuquerque Academy, a private school in Albuquerque.

❖

Freezing Raspberries
Wash berries, drain, the remove the stems, if needed. Place well drained berries on cookie sheets in a single layer and freeze uncovered overnight. The next day, remove the berries from the freezer, and place the loose berries in large, gallon-size freezer bags or glass jars. Serve any time of year by pouring out the quantity of berries needed.

Crème Celeste

1 c. heavy cream
1/2 c. granulated sugar
1 1/2 tsp. plain gelatin
3 T. cold water
1 c. sour cream
1 tsp. vanilla

2 to 3 pt. fresh raspberries or
   2 (10 or 12 oz.) pkgs.
   individually frozen raspberries & 1 (10 or 12 oz.)
   pkg. raspberries frozen in
   juice
Splash of Cointreau (optional)

In saucepan over low heat, heat heavy cream and sugar, stirring constantly until sugar is dissolved.

Soften gelatin in water; stir into cream and sugar. When gelatin is completely dissolved, remove mixture from heat. Softly fold in sour cream. Stir until smooth ONLY. Add vanilla. Pour into an oiled 1-pint mold. Chill 3 hours.

Wash raspberries and drain. Slightly crush with back of spoon to bring out juice. Refrigerate. Just before serving, splash raspberries with Cointreau.

Before serving, unmold créme. Place on beautiful round platter. Spoon raspberries onto top and let juice drizzle down sides of molded créme. Place remaining raspberries around the platter. Slice and serve at table.

Servings: 6 to 8

Extra berries look great in dessert glass around the dessert plate. Very impressive looking, BUT SO EASY!

Gale Doyel   *Albuquerque*

Cold Lemon Soufflé with Raspberry Sauce

1 T. unflavored gelatin	2 tsp. grated lemon rind
1/4 c. cold water	1 1/2 c. sugar
5 eggs, separated	1 c. whipping cream
3/4 c. fresh lemon juice	

Sprinkle gelatin over cold water to soften. Mix egg yolks with lemon juice and rind and 3/4 cup sugar. Place in top of double boiler and cook, stirring constantly until lemon mixture is slightly thickened, about 5 minutes. Remove from heat and stir in gelatin until dissolved. Chill 30 to 40 minutes. Beat egg whites until stiff, gradually adding the remaining 3/4 cup sugar. Whip cream until stiff. Fold egg whites and whipped cream into the yolk mixture until no white streaks remain. Pour into a 2-quart soufflé dish and chill at least 4 hours. Serve with raspberry sauce.

RASPBERRY SAUCE:

2 pkgs. frozen raspberries (in sugar)	2 T. Cointreau

Defrost raspberries and purée in blender until smooth. Strain through a sieve and add Cointreau. Chill.

Servings: 6 to 8

Nadyne Bicknell   *Albuquerque*

Nadyne is a government and community leader active in city and county planning efforts.

❖

Planting Raspberries
Planting is generally done after all danger of frost damage has passed. Although the cost of using tissue-cultured plants is much higher than bareroot stock, these plants usually exhibit greater vigor, are more uniform in size, and have greater growth survival rates.

Wine Jelly

This is a modern interpretation of Thomas Jefferson's recipe.*

2 env. unflavored gelatin	1 pt. wine (Madeira, red
1/2 c. cold water	Burgundy, or sherry)
2 c. strained raspberries	Strained juice of 3 lemons
3/4 to 1 c. sugar	Fresh fruit for garnish
Pinch of salt	

Dissolve 2 envelopes of gelatin in 1/2 cup cold water. Add this to the fruit juice, which has been brought to a boil. Add sugar to taste and a pinch of salt; let cool. Next, add the pint of wine and lemon juice.

Pour into mold that has been chilled. Set in the refrigerator for at least 2 hours. Unmold and serve cold. Decorate with fresh fruits that have been rolled in confectioners' sugar.

*Thomas Jefferson's original recipe is as follows:
"Take 4 calves feet and wash them well without taking off the hoofs.These feet must be well boiled the day before they are wanted. Let them cool in order to take off the greese. After taking off the greese put the jelly in a casserolle. Put there 4 ounces sugar, cloves, nutmeg. Boil all together. Take 6 whites of eggs, the juice of 6 lemons, a pint of milk, a pint of Madiera. Stir all together. Pour into the jelly and boil it. Taste it to see if sweet enough, if not, add powdered sugar. Strain it 2 or 3 times thru' flannel till clear. Put in glasses or moulds."

Thomas Jefferson   *Monticello, VA*

Thomas Jefferson was one of the greatest gourmets to occupy the Executive Mansion. He was also a gentleman farmer and an ardent gardener. According to the records he kept, one of his garden crops was raspberries.

Frozen Desserts

Frosty Raspberry Squares

3/4 c. margarine
1 1/2 c. flour

1/2 c. brown sugar
3/4 c. chopped walnuts

Heat oven to 350°. Melt margarine in a 13x9-inch pan. Spread evenly along bottom of pan. Mix other ingredients and add to margarine. Bake 20 minutes. Stir every 5 minutes. After 20 minutes, remove 1/3 cup of mixture for topping; set aside.

FILLING:
2 egg whites
2/3 c. sugar
2 T. fresh lemon juice

1 (10 oz.) pkg. frozen raspberries, partially thawed
1 c. heavy cream, whipped

In a medium-size bowl, mix egg whites, sugar, lemon juice, and raspberries. Beat 10 minutes at high speed. Fold whipped cream into the mixture. Press down crumbs in a 9x13-inch pan. Add raspberry mixture. Sprinkle the reserved crumbs on top. Freeze. Cover with plastic wrap.

Time: 20 minutes
Temperature: 350°
Servings: 12

Char Brebach   *Albuquerque*

Washing Raspberries
Ripe raspberries are very delicate. Look them over and remove all imperfect berries.
You can wash your berries prior to storage if thoroughly drained on paper toweling.
Or, wash berries just before using. Either way, cover dry berries lightly and
refrigerate till needed.

Raspberry Flummery

1 qt. raspberries
3/4 c. water
1 c. sugar

3 egg whites
2 c. whipping (heavy) cream

Crush and strain raspberries through 2 thicknesses of cheese-cloth to produce about 1 cup of juice. Discard the remaining pulp. Boil water and sugar to about 230° or until syrup makes a 2-inch thread when dropped from a spoon. Whip the egg whites until they are stiff, not dry. Pour the syrup over the egg whites in a slow stream. Whip constantly until cool. Fold in juice.

In a separate bowl, whip cream until thick, not stiff. Fold the cream lightly into the other ingredients. Place in foil-covered refrigerator trays and freeze for 6 hours, making sure to beat the mixture well every 2 hours while it is freezing. (For best texture, do not store mixture for more than 24 hours.)

Flummery may be served in custard cups, topped with fresh raspberries; or layered with a raspberry sauce in stemmed parfait glasses.

QUICK RASPBERRY SAUCE:
1/4 c. sugar
1 c. raspberries

1 T. cornstarch

Mix ingredients. Heat in the microwave for about 1 minute or until mixture starts to thicken.

A "flummery" is much like a mousse and was made during colonial times.

Servings: 7 to 9

Kim Corwin   *Albuquerque*

Kim Corwin is a member of the board of Very Special Arts New Mexico. He is the Co-Director of the "Story Sign Theatre".

131

Frozen Layered Dessert

2 c. graham cracker crumbs
3/4 c. heavy cream
1 c. confectioners' sugar
1/8 lb. butter
1 egg
1 c. raspberries

Cover bottom of an 8-inch pie pan with 1 cup graham cracker crumbs. Whip heavy cream. Spread 1/2 over crumbs. Mix together powdered sugar, butter, and egg. Add a layer of this mixture. Add a layer of fresh raspberries, sweetened to taste. Add rest of whipped cream. Cover with more graham cracker crumbs. Freeze. Set out briefly before serving.

Servings: 8

Richard J. Waite   *Portales*

Richard Waite is from Eastern New Mexican University, located in Portales, NM.

Raspberry Piña Colada Sherbet

1 (8 3/4 oz.) can cream of
  coconut
1 1/2 c. milk
1 c. pineapple juice
1/2 c. puréed & strained
  raspberries
1/4 c. sugar

Combine coconut cream, milk, pineapple juice, raspberry purée, and sugar. Following the directions for your ice cream maker, stir and freeze.

Servings: 1 quart

Joy Jeffrey   *Albuquerque*

Frambuesas Media-Borrachas

(Half-Drunk Raspberries)

1 pt. fresh raspberries,
   cleaned
1/4 c. sugar
1 orange, thinly sliced

1 pt. vanilla ice cream
3 T. blackberry brandy
3 T. Grand Marnier
3 T. tequila

Place raspberries and sugar in a medium-size skillet over low heat. Stir at every step, using a large spoon. After 2 to 3 minutes, place the orange slices and the ensuing juice in the skillet. Raise the heat to medium. After 1 or 2 minutes add the brandy, Grand Marnier, and tequila. Step back a bit, while maintaining your hand on the skillet. Raise the temperature to high. After about 20 to 30 seconds pull the skillet back a bit so that the vapors from the alcohol ignite. This will create a flaming "jubilee" style dessert. Turn off the heat. The raspberry mixture should remain ignited. Now spoon the mixture over the ice cream which was previously dished out equally in four Bolla Grande stem glasses.

EXTREME CAUTION MUST BE USED WHEN MAKING A FLAMING DESSERT. IF YOU HAVE NOT SEEN THE PROCESS OR DON'T FEEL CONFIDENT, THEN YOU CAN DO THE ABOVE RECIPE AT LOW HEAT AND ELIMINATE THE FLAMBÉ. ALWAYS BE AWARE THAT THE ALCOHOL CAN SELF-IGNITE.

Servings: 4

Stuart Ashman   *Santa Fe*

Stuart Ashman is the Curator of the Governor's Gallery at the State Capitol in Santa Fe, New Mexico.

♥Historic Raspberry Ice

1 pt. raspberries
1 1/2 pt. sugar

1 pt. water

Squeeze the juice out of the raspberries and strain well. Add sugar and mix well. Add water. Freeze the same as ice cream.

Lynn Koenig, **Artesia Daily Press**   *Artesia*

Lynn Koenig does historic research and thought this was an interesting old recipe. It comes from the August 18, 1887 edition of the Dodge City, Kansas, Times.

Raspberries Romanoff

1 pt. vanilla ice cream, whipped   2 pt. raspberries
1 pt. heavy cream, whipped   6 T. Cointreau

Combine whipped ice cream, heavy cream, raspberries, and Cointreau. Serve immediately in individual dessert dishes.

Servings: 4 to 6

Sally Burchell   *Albuquerque*

♥Diabetic Raspberry Sorbet

3/4 c. cold water   1 ripe banana, sliced
1 env. unflavored gelatin   2/3 c. frozen, sugarless apple
2 egg whites   concentrate, thawed
2 (10 oz.) pkgs. frozen   Fresh raspberries (or straw-
   unsweetened raspberries,   berries or blueberries)
   thawed (can substitute   4 fresh mint sprigs
   strawberries or blueberries)

Place water in medium saucepan. Sprinkle gelatin over water and let soften 5 minutes. Place over low heat and cook, stirring, until gelatin is dissolved.

In mixing bowl, beat egg whites until stiff. Stir whites into gelatin mixture and cook, stirring constantly, over low heat for 3 to 5 minutes or until mixture is thickened. Remove from heat. Place thawed berries, banana, and apple concentrate in food processor and purée. Stir purée into egg white-gelatin mixture and mix well. Pour into shallow metal pan and freeze for 1 hour, or until almost set. Turn sorbet into a bowl and beat with an electric mixer until smooth, or place in a food processor and process until smooth. Return mixture to pan and freeze for 1 hour longer. If mixture is still grainy, beat again with mixer or in processor. Place in freezer container and freeze until solid. Remove from freezer 15 minutes before serving and let soften at room temperature. Scoop into serving dishes and top with fresh berries and mint.

Servings: 4 (1 generous pint)

Joy Jeffrey   *Albuquerque*

Raspberry Frozen Yogurt

1 env. unflavored gelatin	2 c. sugar
1/2 c. cold water	3 (16 oz.) ctn. (6 c.) plain
2 (10 oz.) pkg. frozen red	yogurt
raspberries, thawed	

In a small saucepan, soften unflavored gelatin in cold water. Cook and stir over low heat until gelatin dissolves. In large bowl, combine gelatin mixture, undrained raspberries, sugar, and 1 cup yogurt. Stir in remaining yogurt. Cover and chill overnight. Pour into 4-quart ice cream freezer. Freeze according to manufacturer's directions.

Servings: 2 1/2 quarts

Gloria K. Thompson   *Shiprock*

♥Raspberry Ice

1 pt. fresh raspberries	2 T. orange juice (or 1 T.
3/4 c. sugar	lemon juice, if preferred)
1/2 c. water	2 egg whites, stiffly beaten
	Few grains of salt

Add sugar to raspberries and crush. Heat slowly and cook for 5 minutes. Add water; strain, cool, and add orange or lemon juice. Pour into freezing tray and freeze until quite firm. Remove to chilled bowl and whip until light. Add salt to stiffly beaten egg whites. Fold the 2 mixtures together well and return quickly to tray and finish freezing.

Serve in parfait glasses or sherbet glasses that have been chilled. Delicious with poultry or fish, or as a dessert.

Servings: 8

Peggy Ritchie   *Albuquerque*

Tortoni
(Almond-Flavored Frozen Custard)

TORTONI:

2 egg yolks
1/2 c. powdered sugar
1 tsp. almond extract
2 egg whites
1/4 tsp. salt

1 c. heavy cream, whipped
1 (5 oz.) can (or 1 heaping c.)
   toasted slivered almonds,
   coarsely chopped

In small bowl, with egg beater or electric mixer, beat egg yolks with sugar and almond extract until smooth and light in color. In medium bowl, with clean beaters, beat egg whites with salt just until stiff peaks form. Gently fold egg yolk mixture and whipped cream into egg whites until well combined.

Sprinkle half of almonds in the bottom of a foil-lined ice cube tray and pour the mixture on top of the almonds. Sprinkle remaining almonds on top. Freeze until firm, 3 to 4 hours. To serve, remove Tortoni from tray. Cut into 10 pieces and top with Cardinal Sauce.

CARDINAL SAUCE:

1 (10 oz.) pkg. frozen raspberries, thawed
1 (10 oz.) pkg. frozen strawberry halves, thawed

2 tsp. cornstarch
1 tsp. grated lemon peel
1 tsp. lemon juice

Drain raspberries and strawberries, reserving liquid from both. In medium saucepan, combine reserved liquids with cornstarch, lemon peel, and lemon juice. Bring to a boil, stirring constantly. Reduce heat. Simmer, uncovered, stirring occasionally, 5 minutes. Remove from heat. Stir in fruit. Refrigerate, covered, until well chilled, at least 2 hours. Serve over frozen Tortoni.

Servings: 10

Gail Murray   *Albuquerque*

Frozen Raspberry Mousse

1 (10 oz.) pkg. frozen rasp-
    berries in syrup
1 c. heavy cream, whipped

1 c. raspberry yogurt
1 egg white, beaten stiff
1/4 c. sugar

Thaw raspberries and purée in blender. Strain to remove seeds if you wish. Add purée to whipped cream and fold in yogurt. Beat egg white to soft peak stage, slowly adding sugar while beating. Fold egg white and sugar mixture into raspberry mixture, blending well. Spoon into 4-cup mold and cover. Freeze, until firm. Remove from freezer half hour or more before serving and put in refrigerator. Unmold and drizzle with sauce.

MELBA SAUCE:

1 (10 oz.) pkg. frozen rasp-
    berries with syrup
1 (12 oz.) pkg. frozen peaches
    with syrup

1 T. cornstarch
1 T. water
2 T. kirsch (cherry brandy)

Defrost and purée fruits. Combine with cornstarch and water, and cook until thick and clear; strain. Stir in kirsch. Chill.

Servings: 8

Nadyne Bicknell   *Albuquerque*

Raspberries on a Cloud

2 egg yolks
1/2 c. honey
2 egg whites
1 1/2 c. heavy cream

1/4 tsp. almond extract
Fresh raspberries (or thawed
    frozen raspberries)

Beat the egg yolks until light. Add the honey and heat in a double boiler until thick. Then chill.

Beat egg whites until stiff. Whip cream. Add almond extract. Fold egg white/cream mixture into chilled egg yolk/honey mixture. Freeze until firm (3 to 4 hours). Serve in sherbet or stemmed glasses. Pour raspberries over individual servings. A liqueur such as kirsch, Cointreau, or Chambord, may also top the clouds.

Joy Jeffrey   *Albuquerque*

Cakes and Cobblers

Chile-Berry Frozen Cheesecake

CRUST:

2 c. graham cracker crumbs

1/3 c. sugar

1 tsp. cinnamon

1/3 c. butter, melted

Combine all the ingredients and blend. Then press firmly over bottom and sides of a buttered 8-inch springform pan. Chill.

FILLING:

16 oz. cream cheese

1 qt. frozen raspberry yogurt

3/4 c. raspberry preserves
    (preferably seedless)

1 c. fresh raspberries

1/4 c. green chile jam

2 1/2 oz. frozen green chile,
    thawed

1/2 c. heavy cream

Let the frozen yogurt soften. Beat cream cheese until soft and then add in the yogurt until completely blended. Spoon 1/4 of the mixture into the crust. In a separate bowl, mix together the raspberry preserves, the green chile jam, and the 1 1/2 ounces of green chile. Drizzle 1/4 of this mixture evenly over the yogurt/cream cheese blend. Repeat this layering 3 more times, but do not spread the final layer of preserves on top. First, freeze the cake, and when it is firm, it will be easier to spread on the final layer of the preserves. Now take the heavy cream, whip, and decorate!

Servings: 10 to 12

This was a finalist in the 1992 Haute Cuisine Contest held by Kistler Collister's of Albuquerque.

Laura Peck   *Albuquerque*

Chris's Raspberry Cheese Cake

CRUST:

20 graham crackers

2 T. sugar

1 1/2 tsp. cinnamon

6 T. melted butter

Roll out graham crackers until fine. Add sugar, cinnamon, and melted butter. Mix and pat into a 9-inch pie pan.

FILLING:

2 lg. & 1 sm. pkgs. cream cheese

1 c. sugar

4 eggs

1/2 tsp. vanilla

Cream cream cheese with 1 cup sugar. Add eggs, one at a time. Mix thoroughly after each egg. Mixing must be done by hand. Add vanilla. Pour into crust-lined pan. Bake 40 to 45 minutes at 350°. Remove from oven. Reset oven to 500°.

TOPPING:

1 pt. sour cream

3 T. sugar

1/2 tsp. vanilla

Mix sour cream with sugar and vanilla. Put on top of cheesecake. Bake for about 5 to 6 minutes or until you see sides of sour cream mixture bubble. Refrigerate 24 hours.

GLAZE:

1 T. cornstarch

1/4 c. water

1/3 c. light corn syrup

1/2 c. slightly crushed raspberries

Stir together cornstarch, water, and corn syrup until smooth. Add raspberries, stirring constantly. Bring to a boil over medium heat. Boil for 1 minute until thick. When cool, spoon over cheesecake.

Time: Cake: 40 to 45 minutes; Topping: 5 to 6 minutes
Temperature: Cake: 350°; Topping: 500°
Servings: 8

While not a major cheesecake fan, Chris loves raspberries and so, the glaze is his favorite part.

Chris Schueler and Karen Clifford   *Albuquerque*

Continued on following page.

Continued from preceding page.

Chris Schueler is the creator of the Emmy award-winning "TV 101" on Channel 13 in Albuquerque. This is a continuing program in which high school students produce, direct, edit, and videotape their own news features about themselves and concerns.
Karen Clifford submitted this wonderful dessert because it is one of Chris's favorites.

Raspberry Pandowdy

5 c. raspberries, washed & drained	2 tsp. baking powder
2 T. cornstarch	1/2 tsp. salt
1 tsp. cinnamon	1 lg. egg
1/2 tsp. nutmeg	1/2 c. milk
1/2 c. sugar	1/4 c. butter, softened
1 1/4 c. unsifted flour	Additional sugar & nutmeg (optional)

Heat oven to 375°.

Toss raspberries with cornstarch, cinnamon, nutmeg, and 2 tablespoons sugar; set aside. In a medium bowl, combine flour, remaining sugar, baking powder, and salt. Make a well in the center. Add egg, milk, and butter. Mix until well combined. Divide raspberry mixture into six 1-cup custard cups or individual soufflé dishes. Top berries with pandowdy batter. If desired, sprinkle with a little sugar and nutmeg. Bake on a cookie sheet until top is golden brown—about 35 to 40 minutes. Serve warm.

Time: 35 to 40 minutes
Temperature: 375°
Servings: 6

The name pandowdy is said to have come from the tradition of breaking the crust with a spoon and mixing it into the fruit filling before serving. Dowdying made the dessert less attractive, but moistened the crisp crust.

Eva Clarke   *Ruidoso*

Eva is the Very Special Arts New Mexico coordinator in Ruidoso and worked on the "Start with the Arts" program that produced some of the art featured in this book.

Raspberry Cobbler

COBBLER BATTER:

3/4 c. sugar
3 T. margarine, room
    temperature
1/2 c. milk

1 tsp. baking powder
1 c. flour
1/2 tsp. salt

Combine ingredients and set aside.

FRUIT LAYER:

4 to 6 c. raspberries
1/2 to 1 c. sugar (omit if using
    frozen, sweetened
    raspberries)

1 c. sugar
1 T. cornstarch
Pinch of salt
1 c. boiling water

Place 4 to 6 cups fresh raspberries in a 9x9-inch baking dish. Sprinkle with 1/2 to 1 cup sugar. (If using frozen sweetened raspberries, omit the sugar.) Put mixed cobbler ingredients over raspberries. Combine sugar, cornstarch, and salt. Sprinkle mixture over cobbler. Then pour boiling water over all and bake at 350° for 1 hour, or until toothpick comes out clean. Yummy!

Time: 1 hour
Temperature: 350°
Servings: 5 to 6

Margaret Prina   *Albuquerque*

Eating Raspberries
Sprinkle on dry cereal and put the whole thing in the microwave for 1 to 1 1/2 minutes at medium. Delicious!

Quick and Easy
Raspberry Cobbler

1 c. sugar
1 c. flour
1 tsp. baking powder
Pinch of salt

3 T. margarine, melted
3/4 c. milk
1 to 2 c. raspberries

Combine sugar, flour, baking powder, salt, margarine, and milk. Pour into an 8x8-inch baking pan. Place the raspberries on top of the batter. Bake 35 to 40 minutes at 350°.

Time: 35 to 40 minutes
Temperature: 350°
Servings: 6 to 8

Garnish with your favorite frozen yogurt or ice cream and top with fresh raspberries.

Bettye Bobroff   *Belen*

Bettye Bobroff is the Director of Personnel for the Belen, New Mexico public school system.

Peach Raspberry Kuchen

SHELL:

1 stick (1/2 c.) unsalted butter
1/3 c. granulated sugar
2 T. light brown sugar
1 lg. egg
1/2 tsp. vanilla

1/4 tsp. almond extract
1 1/2 c. all-purpose flour
1 tsp. double-acting baking
   powder
3/4 tsp. salt

In a small saucepan, cook butter over moderate heat until it is golden brown. Be careful not to let it burn. Let it cool. Chill it until it is no longer liquid. (The butter may be browned 1 day in advance and kept covered and chilled. Let the butter soften at room temperature before using.)

In a bowl, cream together browned butter and granulated sugar. Beat in egg, vanilla, and almond extract. Sift flour, baking powder, and salt into the bowl. Beat until it is just combined. Chill the dough for 30 minutes and press it onto the bottom and side of a 9-inch tart pan with a removable fluted rim.

TOPPING:

2 firm, ripe peaches
2 T. sugar
1/2 pt. raspberries

1/4 c. currant jelly, melted &
   cooled

In a saucepan of boiling water, blanch peaches for 1 minute. Drain them and refresh them under cold water. Peel them and halve them. Cut 3 of the halves into 1/8-inch-thick slices. Reserve the remaining half for another use. Arrange the slices decoratively, overlapping them slightly in the shell. Sprinkle them with sugar. Bake the kuchen in the lower third of a preheated 375° oven for 20 minutes. Arrange the raspberries decoratively over the peaches and bake the kuchen for 10 more minutes. Transfer the kuchen to a rack. Brush the fruit with jelly. Let the kuchen cool for 15 minutes. Remove the rim of the pan and serve the kuchen warm or at room temperature.

Time: 30 minutes
Temperature: 375°
Servings: 10 to 12

Marilyn Salman, Salman Ranch   *LaCueva*

♥Fresh Orange Shortcake
for the '90's

BISCUITS:

2 1/4 c. reduced-fat baking &
  pancake mix
2 T. + 1 tsp. sugar
Grated peel of 1 orange

1/3 c. fresh-squeezed orange
  juice
1/3 c. lowfat milk

In large bowl, combine baking mix, 2 tablespoons sugar, and grated orange peel. Add orange juice and milk. Mix until soft dough forms. Place on flour-dusted surface. Roll in flour and shape into a ball. Knead gently 8 to 10 minutes. Pat or roll into 6x4-inch rectangle. With floured knife, cut into six 2-inch squares. Place 2 inches apart on ungreased cookie sheet. Sprinkle tops with remaining 1 teaspoon sugar. Bake at 425° for 8 to 11 minutes, until just lightly browned on top; cool.

FRESH ORANGE FILLING:

2 to 3 T. raspberry fruit spread
  or jam
1 (1.3 oz.) env. whipped topping
  mixed to yield 2 c. topping
1/2 c. lowfat milk, cold

Grated peel from 1/2 orange
4 to 5 oranges, peeled, cut
  into 1/2 cartwheel slices
Fresh raspberries & mint for
  garnish (opt.)

Slice biscuits in half crosswise. Spread each biscuit half lightly with raspberry jam. In small deep bowl, with electric mixer, beat mixed whipped topping and cold milk at high speed for about 4 minutes, or until mixture thickens and soft peaks form. Stir in orange peel. Arrange orange slices and whipped topping on bottom half of each biscuit. Top with remaining biscuit-half and additional whipped topping. Garnish with mint and raspberry, if desired.

Time: 8 to 11 minutes
Temperature: 425°
Servings: 6

Beth Capps   *Las Vegas*

Beth Capps is a volunteer for Very Special Arts New Mexico in Las Vegas.

Raspberry Rhapsody

1 (12 oz.) pkg. frozen raspberries, thawed
1 (3 oz.)m pkg. raspberry
gelatin
1 c. boiling water

1/2 c. cold water
1 pt. whipping cream
1/3 c. powdered sugar
1 lg. angel food cake
1 T. cornstarch

Drain raspberries, reserving juice. Mix gelatin with boiling water. Add cold water. Chill until almost set. Whip until fluffy. Whip cream with sugar until it stands in soft peaks. Fold into gelatin. Fold in raspberries. Remove brown crust from cake and break into small pieces. In angel food cake pan, alternate layers of gelatin mixture and cake, beginning and ending with gelatin mixture. Chill overnight. Combine raspberry juice and cornstarch; cook over moderate heat, stirring constantly until mixture thickens. Cool. Unmold the cake onto plate. Drizzle juice mixture on top and sides of cake.

You may bake your own angel food cake, or use a purchased one from the store. This is DELICIOUS and well worth the effort.

Servings: 10 to 12

Sue Jackson   *Albuquerque*

Forgotten Cake

6 egg whites
1/2 to 1 c. sugar

1 1/2 tsp. vanilla
1 pt. raspberries

Preheat oven to 450°.

Beat egg whites until soft peaks. Gradually add sugar and continue beating. Add vanilla. Pour into pan. (Use an 8-inch square or round cake pan.

Put cake in the oven and turn oven off. Do not open the oven until the next morning. Serve with raspberries and whipped cream.

Time; Overnight
Temperature: 450°
Servings: 6

Esther Mailander   *Albuquerque*

♥Shortcake

2 1/2 c. whole wheat pastry flour	1 c. honey
3 1/2 tsp. baking powder	1/2 c. sesame oil
1 tsp. salt	1 1/2 c. water
2 T. wheat germ	1 T. vanilla
	2/3 c. chopped raspberries

Sift dry ingredients, adding wheat germ after sifting. Mix honey, sesame oil, water, and vanilla, and beat into the dry ingredients. Mix raspberries into batter. Pour into a greased 9x9-inch pan. Bake at 325° until done (cake will spring back when pressed down).

Time: 30 minutes
Temperature: 325°
Servings: 6 to 8

Yogi Bhajan   *Española*

Yogi Bhajan is the Head Minister for Sikh Dharma in the Western Hemisphere, Asia, and Asia Minor.

Raspberry Dream Cake

1 homemade or store-bought angel food cake	1 med. ctn. frozen whipped topping
2 c. fresh raspberries, or medium-size jar raspberry preserves	

Slice cake into 3 layers. Use half the raspberry preserves to spread preserves on each layer. Reassemble cake. Fold remaining preserves into thawed whipped topping. Frost cake with mixture. Refrigerate several hours.

Servings: 8 to 10

Marjorie Correll   *Las Vegas*

Kathy Baker's Raspberry Cream Cheese Cake

CRUST:
2 1/4 c. all-purpose flour
3/4 c. sugar
3/4 c. (1 1/2 sticks) margarine, chilled

1/2 tsp. baking powder
1/2 tsp. baking soda
3/4 c. sour cream
1 egg
1 tsp. almond extract

Preheat oven to 350°. Combine flour and sugar in a large bowl. Cut in margarine and mix to resemble coarse crumbs. Set aside 1 cup of crumb mixture for topping. To remaining mixture, add baking powder, soda, sour cream, egg, and almond extract. Blend well and chill for about 15 to 20 minutes, while you prepare filling and topping.

FILLING:
1 (8 oz.) pkg. cream cheese, softened
1/4 c. sugar
1 egg

1 to 2 tsp. grated lemon rind
1/2 c. raspberry preserves or fruit spread
1 T. rum

Combine cream cheese, sugar, egg, and lemon zest; beat well. Set aside. In separate bowl, combine raspberry preserves and rum.

TOPPING:
1/2 c. sliced almonds

Sprinkling of confectioners' sugar, if desired

Combine reserved crumb mixture and sliced almonds in small bowl.

PREPARATION:
Grease and flour a springform pan. Lightly grease fingers and press crust batter over bottom and 2 inches up side of pan. Pour cream cheese mixture evenly over batter, then pour raspberry mixture on top and spread evenly. Sprinkle reserved crumb mixture and almonds over top. Bake at 350° for 50 to 60 minutes, or until cream cheese filling is set and crust is deep golden brown. Cool 15 minutes, then remove sides of pan. Sprinkle a light dusting of confectioners' sugar on top, if desired.

Continued on following page.

Continued from preceding page.

For extra fancy preparation, purée 2 boxes of raspberries plus a dash of lemon juice. Pour a "lake" of purée in the bottom of each dessert plate. Place wedge of cake on top and decorate with extra fresh raspberries, lemon slices and a sprig of mint.

"This delicious birthday cake, tea cake, or elegant dessert cake is dedicated to Juanita Finke Dorris, a wonderful cook and the head of the Dorris clan, which has been my second family in Albuquerque for over 30 years. The recipe was inspired by the lovely women in my favorite bookstore, The Bookworks, in the North Valley where we make our home."

Temperature: 350°
Time: 1 hour
Servings: 12 to 16

Kathy Baker   *Los Angeles, CA*

Kathy Baker is the star of the hit TV series, Picket Fences. *When she is not filming, she lives in Albuquerque.*

❖

A Quick and Elegant Raspberry Dessert
Fill a crystal gobler with fresh raspberries. Top with a dollop of sour cream and sprinkle with brown sugar.

Bars & Cookies

Doogie Howser's Raspberry-Oatmeal Squares

1 1/4 c. whole wheat pastry
    flour
1 1/4 c. rolled oats
1/3 c. brown sugar

2/3 c. liquid margarine
3/4 c. "fruit only" raspberry
    preserves

In food processor, combine flour, oats, sugar, and margarine. Press 1/2 of mixture into an 8x8-inch cooking pan sprayed with cooking spray. Spread with preserves. Press remaining mixture evenly over preserves. Bake at 350° for 30 minutes; cool. Cut into squares.

Time: 30 minutes
Temperature: 350°
Yield: 16 cookies

These are good, easy, and healthy!

Neil Patrick Harris   *Los Angeles, CA*

Neil Patrick Harris is the star of the television series, Doogie Howser, M.D. *He attended La Cueva High School in Albuquerque.*

Raspberry Oatmeal Bars

1 pkg. yellow cake mix	1 (12 oz.) jar raspberry jam
2 1/2 c. quick-cooking oats	1 T. water
3/4 c. margarine or butter, melted	

Combine cake mix and oats. Stir in melted margarine until mixture is crumbly. Put about 3 cups of mixture in a 9x13-inch pan and press firmly. Combine jam and water and spoon over crumb mixture; spread evenly. Cover with remaining crumb mixture; make top even by patting firmly.

Bake at 375° for 20 minutes. Cool before cutting into bars.

Time: 20 minutes
Temperature: 375°
Servings: 10 to 12

Betty Garrett   *Albuquerque*

Betty submitted this recipe to Art Schreiber's radio talk show when he was asking for recipes for this cookbook. He doesn't cook, but loves to eat, so needed his listeners' help.

Raspberry Bars

3/4 c. margarine	1 1/2 c. old-fashioned or quick
1 c. packed brown sugar	oats, uncooked
1 1/2 c. all-purpose flour	1 (10 oz.) jar raspberry
1 tsp. salt	preserves
1/2 tsp. baking soda	

Cream margarine and brown sugar until light and fluffy. Combine all dry ingredients. Add to creamed mixture and mix well. Press half of crumb mixture into greased 9x13-inch baking pan. Spread with preserves. Sprinkle with remaining crumb mixture.

Bake at 400° for 20 to 25 minutes. Cool and cut.

Time: 20 to 25 minutes
Temperature: 400°
Yield: 1 1/2 to 3 dozen

Jane Thomas   *Santa Fe*

Challenge New Mexico offers support, advocacy and recreational programs to people with physical or mental challenges. It also provides office space for Very Special Arts New Mexico in Santa Fe. Jane Thomas serves on Challenge New Mexico's board.

Raspberry Almond Squares

1 1/2 c. sifted flour
1/2 c. sugar
1/2 tsp. baking powder
1/2 tsp. cinnamon
1/2 c. butter

1/2 c. ground almonds
1 egg
1/2 tsp. almond extract
3/4 c. raspberry jam

Preheat oven to 350°.

In medium-size bowl, sift together flour, sugar, baking powder, and cinnamon. Cut in butter. Stir in egg, almond extract, and ground almonds. Divide dough in half. Spread half of dough in lightly greased 8-inch square pan. Spread other half on wax paper that has been placed in another 8-inch square pan. Cover dough in greased pan with raspberry jam; top with remaining square of dough. Bake for 40 minutes. Cool.

ICING (optional):
3/4 c. confectioners' sugar

3 tsp. milk
1/4 tsp. almond extract

Mix all ingredients. Drizzle over cooled cake. Cut cake in squares.

Time: 40 minutes
Temperature: 350°
Yield: 16 squares

Patricia A. Scott   *Albuquerque*

Patricia Scott is the Executive Director of the National Kidney Foundation of New Mexico.

❖

Raspberry Facial by Camilla Trujillo
Camillo Trujillo thinks the best way to eat fresh raspberries is just off the plant. "I do like to make a facial with them, though," she says. "Take a handful of fresh raspberries. Crush gently. Rub the juice over neck and face. Allow to dry 10 to 15 minutes. Wash off with cool water. Brings the color right to your cheeks."
Comments: This probably is best done in and near a lake or pond and with a black bathing suit!

Raspberry Jewels

2 c. flour
1 c. butter, soft
1/2 c. sugar
1/8 tsp. salt
1 egg yolk, beaten

1/2 c. raspberry jam
1/4 c. blanched slivered
    almonds
1/2 tsp. vanilla

Combine flour, butter, sugar, and salt with a pastry blender. Add egg yolk and work with hands until it forms a ball. Divide into thirds. Shape each portion into a 1x12-inch strip. Place strips about 4 inches apart on an ungreased cookie sheet. Make a depression about 1/2-inch deep down the center of each strip. Combine jam, almonds, and vanilla. Spread 1/3 of jam mixture in center of each strip. Refrigerate on tray 30 minutes to firm up. Bake at 350° for 20 to 25 minutes until light brown. Cut each strip into 1-inch diagonal pieces. Cool on wire racks. Remove and serve.

A beautiful and delicious cookie, perfect for teas and special family meals.

Time: 20 to 25 minutes
Temperature: 350°
Yield: 24 bars

Kathy Sabin   *Roswell*

Kathy Sabin is the Curator of Education and the Librarian at the Roswell Museum and Art Center in Roswell, New Mexico.

Vienna Chocolate Bars

2 sticks butter (1/2 lb. softened)
1 1/4 c. sugar
2 1/2 c. flour
1 (10 oz.) jar raspberry jam or
    jelly

1 c. semisweet chocolate bits
1/4 tsp. salt
4 egg whites
2 c. finely chopped almonds

Cream butter with 1/4 cup sugar. Add egg yolks and beat. Add flour and knead with fingers. Pat batter onto a greased 10x15-inch cookie sheet. Bake 15 to 20 minutes at 350° until lightly browned. Remove from oven. Spread with jelly or jam, and top with chocolate bits.

Continued on following page.

Continued from preceding page.

Beat egg whites with salt until stiff. Fold in remaining cup of sugar and nuts. Gently spread on top of jam and chocolate. Bake for 20 to 25 minutes at 350°. Cut into squares or bars while warm.

Time: 35 to 45 minutes
Temperature: 350°
Servings: 4 dozen

Lois Dittmer   *Albuquerque*

Raspberry Coconut Layer Bars

1 2/3 c. graham cracker crumbs
1/2 c. butter or margarine,
   melted
2 2/3 c. (7 oz. pkg.) flaked
   coconut
1 1/4 c. (14 oz. can) sweetened
   condensed milk

1 c. red raspberry jam or
   preserves
1/3 c. finely chopped pecans,
   toasted
1/2 c. semisweet chocolate
   morsels, melted
1/4 c. (1 1/2 oz.) white chocolate baking bar, melted

In medium bowl, combine graham cracker crumbs and butter. Spread evenly over bottom of a 13x9-inch baking pan, pressing to make compact crust. Sprinkle coconut over crust. Pour sweetened condensed milk evenly over coconut. Bake in preheated 350° oven for 20 to 25 minutes, or until lightly browned. Cool. Spread jam over coconut layer; chill 3 to 4 hours. Sprinkle with pecans. Drizzle melted dark chocolate, then melted white chocolate over top layer to make lace effect; chill. Cut into 3 x 1 1/2-inch bars.

Time: 20 to 25 minutes
Temperature: 350°
Yield: 24 bars

Joy Jeffrey   *Albuquerque*

Raspberry Chews

3/4 c. (1 1/2 sticks) butter or
 margarine
1/4 c. sugar
2 eggs, separated
1/2 c. sifted regular flour

1/2 c. sugar
1 c. chopped walnuts
1 c. raspberry preserves
1/2 c. flaked coconut

Cream butter or margarine with 1/4 cup of the sugar until fluffy-light in a medium-size bowl; beat in egg yolks. Stir in flour until blended. Spread evenly in a baking pan, 13x9x2-inches.

Bake in a 350° oven for 15 minutes, or until golden; remove from oven. While layer bakes, beat egg whites until foamy-white and doubled in volume in a small bowl. Beat in remaining 1/2 cup sugar until meringue stands in firm peaks. Fold in walnuts.

Spread raspberry preserves over layer in pan; sprinkle with coconut. Spread meringue over raspberry-coconut layer. Bake in 350° oven for 25 minutes, or until lightly golden; cool. Cut into bars.

Time: 15 minutes, then 25 minutes
Temperature: 350°
Yield: 20 bars

Karen Turner   *Albuquerque*

Raspberry Shortbread Dessert

1 c. butter
2 c. flour
1/2 c. powdered sugar
1 T. cornstarch

1/4 tsp. salt
Sugar to taste
1 qt. raspberries
1 c. whipped cream

Cream butter. Sift together flour, powdered sugar, cornstarch, and salt. Work flour mixture into butter with fingers and press mixture into an 8x12-inch pan. Mark 12 equal squares. Bake at 325° for 25 minutes. Cut through marked squares while still warm; let cool completely. Meanwhile, add sugar to berries and chill. To serve, place equal amounts of whipped cream on each cookie and spoon berries on top of whipped cream.

Time: 25 minutes
Temperature: 325°
Servings: 12

Shannon Marshall   *McAllen, TX*

Raspberry Hamentoschen

4 eggs, beaten
1 c. vegetable oil
1 c. sugar
1 tsp. vanilla
1/2 tsp. salt

1 tsp. baking powder
5 to 5 1/2 c. flour
1 to 2 c. raspberry preserves
   or fruit spread

Mix eggs, oil, sugar, vanilla, salt, and baking powder. Beat lightly. Add flour gradually to form a ball and remove to a floured surface. Knead dough until soft and easy to roll.

Preheat oven to 350°. Lightly grease cookie sheets. Roll out kneaded dough on lightly floured board. Cut out circles (using a glass). Spoon 1 to 2 teaspoons filling (raspberries) in center. Pinch together into a triangle shape. Bake 30 minutes or until light brown.

Time: 30 minutes
Temperature: 350°
Yield: 24

This is a triangle-shaped pastry usually eaten during the Purim holiday. The name Hamentoschen, roughly translated from the Hebrew, means Hamen's hat. According to Jewish tradition, Hamen is the villain of the story which forms the basis for the celebration of the Festival of Purim. The traditional fillings are prune or a poppyseed mixture called "mohn".

Janet Stein Romero   *Las Vegas*

As District Director for Very Special Arts New Mexico in Las Vegas, Janet oversees arts programs for persons with disabilities.

Pies

Raspberry Cloud Pie

2 c. graham cracker crumbs
1/2 c. melted butter
1/2 c. packed brown sugar
1 (3 oz.) pkg. raspberry gelatin
1 1/2 c. hot water

3 c. raspberries
5 1/2 oz. marshmallows
1/2 c. milk
1 env. whipped topping mix,
    prepared

Combine graham cracker crumbs, butter, and brown sugar in bowl; mix well. Reserve 1/4 of the mixture. Press remaining crumb mixture into a 9x13-inch dish. Dissolve gelatin in hot water in a saucepan. Add raspberries. Cook until thickened. Pour over crust. Melt marshmallows in milk in saucepan. Bring to a boil; cool. Fold in whipped topping gently. Spread over filling. Sprinkle remaining crumb mixture on top. Chill in refrigerator.

Wonderful dessert for bridge, patio parties, warm weather. This recipe was given to Dollie by her grandmother.

Servings: 10 to 12

Dollie Lowery   *Albuquerque*

Raspberry Marshmallow Pie

1 env. unflavored gelatin
1/2 c. cold water
1/2 c. sugar
1 tsp. to 1 T. lemon juice
    (depends on sweetness
    desired)

1 (3 oz.) pkg. cream cheese,
    whipped
1 (10 oz.) pkg. frozen rasp-
    berries, thawed
1 pkg. whipped topping
2 c. miniature marshmallows
1 baked pie shell

Soften gelatin in cold water. Stir over low heat until dissolved. Add sugar and lemon juice. While still warm, gradually add this mixture to softened, whipped cream cheese. Fold in raspberries. Chill until thickened. Whip after it is thick and fold in whipped topping and marshmallows. Pour into crust and chill until firm.

Servings: 4 to 6

Carol A. Moore   *Los Alamos*

Raspberry Cream Pie

1 c. sugar
1 c. sour cream, light sour
   cream or yogurt, drained
3 T. flour

1/4 tsp. salt
4 c. fresh raspberries or 16 oz.
   frozen raspberries, thawed
1 (9-inch) unbaked pie shell

Combine sugar, sour cream, flour, and salt; set aside. Place berries in pie shell. Spread cream mixture over berries.

TOPPING:
1/2 c. fine, dry bread crumbs

1/4 c. sugar
2 T. butter, melted

Combine ingredients. Spread over berries and cream mixture. Bake at 375° on lowest oven shelf for 40 to 50 minutes. Serve at room temperature.

Quick and easy when prepared pie shell is used.

Time: 40 to 50 minutes
Temperature: 375°
Servings: 6 to 8

Lyn Hagaman   *Albuquerque*

At one time Lyn Hagaman worked and was well-known as a cooking instructor in Albuquerque. She is now a property consultant.

Yogurt Raspberry Pie

1/2 c. crushed raspberries
2 (8 oz.) ctns. raspberry yogurt

1 (8 oz.) ctn. prepared
   whipped topping
1 graham cracker crust

Thoroughly combine crushed raspberries and yogurt. Fold in whipped topping, blending well. Spoon into crust and freeze 4 hours (or overnight). Remove from freezer and place in refrigerator 1 hour before serving. Decorate top with whole raspberries. Store any leftover pie in freezer.

Servings: 6 to 8

Maddie Soales   *Albuquerque*

Maddie Soales has been a faithful volunteer at the Raspberry Festivals.

Raspberry Patch Pie

PIE CRUST:
Bake a 9-inch pie shell
(see index)

FRUIT MIXTURE:
3 c. fresh lg. raspberries   1/2 c. powdered sugar

Mix and allow to stand 1 hour.

GLAZE:
1 c. raspberries   1 1/2 T. cornstarch
1/2 to 3/4 c. sugar   Whipped cream
1 c. water

Mash berries. Add water and boil 2 minutes. Strain mixture to remove seeds. Add cornstarch and sugar. Cook until clear. Add a few drops of red food coloring if a deeper red is desired. Bake in pie shell. Put sweetened raspberries in shell. (Drain if too much juice has accumulated.) Cover with glaze. Top with whipped cream.

Servings: 12

Char Brebach   *Albuquerque*

Frozen Raspberry Pie

1 (10 oz.) pkg. frozen   1/2 tsp. almond flavoring
    raspberries   Dash of salt
1 c. sugar   1 c. whipping cream, whipped
2 egg whites at room   1/4 c. chopped roasted
    temperature   almonds
1 tsp. lemon juice   1 (9-inch) pie shell, baked

Thaw raspberries. Preserve a few for garnish. Combine raspberries, sugar, egg whites, lemon juice, almond flavoring, and salt. Beat until mixed, 15 minutes, or until stiff. Fold in whipped cream and almonds. Mound in pie shell. Freeze until firm. Garnish with reserved raspberries and sprigs of mint.

Servings: 10

Carmela Bentz   *Las Cruces*

Lemon Ice Cream Pie with Warm Berry Sauce

CRUST:
1/4 c. butter or margarine
1 c. graham cracker crumbs
1 c. finely chopped nuts
2 T. sugar
1/2 tsp. ground cinnamon

Place butter in a 9-inch microwave-proof pie plate. Microwave on MEDIUM (50% POWER) until melted, 2 or 3 minutes. Add crumbs, nuts, sugar, and cinnamon. Stir to mix well. With back of spoon, press mixture against sides and bottom of pie plate to form an even crust. Microwave on HIGH (100% POWER) until set, 1 1/2 minutes to 2 minutes. Allow to cool, then refrigerate crust 15 minutes to chill.

FILLING:
1/2 gal. vanilla ice cream
1/4 c. fresh lemon juice
2 T. grated lemon peel
1 lemon, thinly sliced (optional)

Place ice cream in microwave on DEFROST until ice cream is soft enough to spoon easily, about 1 minute. Spoon ice cream into large bowl and fold in lemon juice and grated lemon peel. Spoon ice cream mixture into prepared crust, rounding top. Cover and freeze at least 1 hour, or overnight, until frozen solid. Just before serving, garnish with lemon slices. Serve with Warm Berry Sauce.

WARM BERRY SAUCE:
2 c. fresh raspberries
2 T. raspberry jam
2 T. fruit-flavored liqueur
     (optional)
1 T. fresh lemon juice

Place berries, jam, liqueur, and lemon juice in a 4-cup glass measure. Microwave on HIGH until just heated through, 4 to 5 minutes, stirring once.

Time: 1 1/2 hours
Servings: 8 to 10

Note: For the calorie-conscious, use ice milk. It gives a lighter texture.

Karen Turner   *Albuquerque*

Mango Raspberry Pie

FILLING:

1 pt. raspberries

2 mangos

1/2 c. sugar, honey, or maple syrup

1/2 c. grated coconut (optional)

Cut mango into 1/2-inch chunks. Mix with raspberries. Sweeten to taste. Add coconut, if desired. Set aside.

CRUST:

1 1/2 c. white flour

1/2 c. wheat germ

2 T. lemon juice or vinegar

2/3 c. butter or margarine

1/4 c. cold water

Blend flour, wheat germ, and lemon juice. Cut butter into pea-size pieces and blend into flour mixture with food processor or pastry knife. Add water as necessary to make dough moist, but not sticky. Divide dough into 2 parts. Roll each to fit 9-inch pie dish. Put 1 crust in bottom. Add fruit mixture. Put top crust on. Bake at 350° for 45 to 60 minutes, or until crust is golden.

Time: 45 minutes

Temperature: 350°

Servings: 8

Will McDonald   *Santa Fe*

Will McDonald is an artist with Special Kids and Special Fathers, a Very Special Arts Program in Santa Fe, New Mexico.

Raspberry Whipped Cream Pie

1 T. unflavored gelatin
1/4 c. cold water
1/2 c. raspberry juice
1/2 c. sugar
1 tsp. salt

2 tsp. lemon juice
1 c. raspberries, mashed
1 1/2 c. heavy cream, whipped
   to stiff peaks
1 baked pie shell

Soak gelatin and water in a medium saucepan for 5 minutes. Then combine juice of raspberries, sugar, salt, and lemon juice; add to gelatin. Heat and stir until gelatin dissolves, about 3 or 4 minutes at medium temperature.

Add raspberries to the mixture and pour in a plastic bowl to chill until thickened, 1/2 hour or so. Fold in whipped cream. Mound mixture into pie shell and chill 2 to 3 hours.

Servings: 6 to 8

Al Martin, Clarity and Mark Howell				*Santa Fe*

The Pinetones is a musical group from Santa Fe, New Mexico. The following note accompanied their recipe:
"If you have good friends to play banjo and fiddle music with, you can make the dessert and put it in the refrigerator to chill for 2 to 3 hours, and play tunes and sing in the meantime, until it's done or you are ready to take a break. New Mexico apricots may be substituted in this recipe to good advantage. Apricot or apple juice may also be substituted. Enjoy! And have fun making music!"

Maggie on Growing Raspberries
Weeds don't make berries, so they can't stay. To reduce her time behind the hoe, Maggie lays black plastic between the rows and covers it with sand. Hoeing is part of gardening, but her tools are seeing less action.

Raspberry Galette

PASTRY:

1 1/2 c. flour	1 rounded T. sugar
Pinch of salt	1 T. water
6 T. butter	1 egg yolk

In mixing bowl, stir flour and salt. With a pastry blender or 2 knives, cut in butter until mixture forms coarse crumbs. Blend water and sugar with yolk in a small bowl. Stir mixture into the flour. Knead lightly to form a dough. Roll dough into a 9-inch circle between 2 sheets of wax paper. Transfer onto a rimless cookie sheet. Press thumb around edge of pastry to flute and form indentations. Prick all over with a fork. Bake at 400° near top of oven for 20 to 25 minutes, or until golden. Transfer onto serving plate and allow to cool.

FILLING:

2 c. raspberries	Whipped cream or whipped
3 rounded T. red currant or	topping
plum jelly	

Place a raspberry on each indentation formed around edge. Arrange rest of fruit in center. Heat jelly until melted. Pour evenly over raspberries and leave to set. Pipe a ring of whipped cream just inside the circle of raspberries placed on the edge of the galette and serve.

Time: 20 to 25 minutes
Temperature: 400°
Servings: 6 to 8

Olga Bezpalko *Socorro*

Mile-High Raspberry Pie

ALMOND PASTRY:

1/4 c. butter
1/4 tsp. salt
2 T. sugar
1 egg yolk

3/4 c. sifted flour
1/4 c. finely chopped
    almonds

Cream butter, salt, and sugar until light and fluffy. Add egg yolk; beat well. Stir in flour and almonds to make a stiff dough. Press into a 9-inch pan. Refrigerate 30 minutes, then bake for 10 minutes at 400°, until golden.

FILLING:

1 (10 or 12 oz.) pkg. frozen
    raspberries; or 2 1/2 c.
    fresh raspberries
1 c. sugar for frozen &
    1 1/3 c. sugar for fresh
    raspberries

1 T. lemon juice
Dash of salt
2 egg whites, room
    temperature
1 c. heavy cream, whipped
1/2 tsp. almond extract

Thaw raspberries if frozen. Place raspberries in large bowl of mixer. Add sugar, lemon juice, salt, and egg whites. Beat 15 minutes, or until stiff. Fold in whipped cream and almond extract. Mound in baked pastry shell. Freeze until firm. Serve.

Time: 10 minutes
Temperature: 400°
Servings: 8

Anne and Heidi Britt, Britt Design Assoc.   *Albuquerque*

Raspberry Delight

CRUST:

2 c. crushed cinnamon crisp graham crackers (12 crackers)

3/4 stick margarine, softened

Mix and line bottom of a 9x12-inch pan. Chill.

FILLING:

1 (8 oz.) pkg. cream cheese

1 c. confectioners' sugar

1 c. chopped pecans

8 oz. nonfat dessert topping

Combine filling ingredients. Spread over crust and chill.

TOPPING:

2 c. raspberries

1/2 c. sugar

Before serving, top with sugared raspberries.

Servings: 8 to 10

Helen Goode   *Las Cruces*

Paula Summar's Favorite Raspberry Recipes

1. Get up early on a Saturday morning during raspberry season. Drive to Salman Ranch. Go in their store and get in line in the back room. Order a dish of homemade vanilla ice cream with raspberries.

2. Take the plastic off a half-pint of raspberries. Rinse the berries gently in a colander. Pour the berries into your favorite bowl. Eat. Share only if you have to.

Paula Summar is the Food Editor of the Albuquerque Journal.

Layered Raspberry Pie

CRUST:

1 1/2 c. vanilla wafer crumbs   1/4 c. butter or margarine,
                                        melted

In a medium-sized bowl, combine vanilla wafer crumbs and melted butter or margarine, and mix together. Reserve 1/4 cup for the topping. Press remainder into the bottom of a 10-inch pie pan.

PIE:

1/2 c. butter or margarine   2 eggs
1 1/2 c. confectioners' sugar

In a medium-sized bowl, cream butter or margarine and gradually add confectioners' sugar. Add eggs, one at a time, and beat the mixture until it is light and fluffy. Spread over crust and chill.

FILLING:

1/2 c. sugar   1 (10 oz.) pkg. frozen
2 T. cornstarch   raspberries, thawed

In a saucepan, combine sugar and cornstarch. Add raspberries and cook over medium heat, stirring constantly, until thick and clear. Allow to cool and then pour over "pie" layer.

TOPPING:

1 c. heavy cream   1 tsp. vanilla extract
1/4 c. confectioners' sugar

In a medium-sized bowl, beat cream until stiff. Fold in sugar and vanilla. Spread over raspberry layer. Sprinkle with reserved crumbs from crust. Chill several hours before serving.

Servings: 6 to 8

Pat Dryden   *Albuquerque*

Pat is very active in Carrie Tingly Hospital activities. Her husband David Dryden is the administrator of Carrie Tingley Hospital.

Tortes

Linzertorte

1 c. butter
1 c. granulated sugar
1 whole egg plus 1 yolk
   (reserve white for glazing)
1 tsp. grated lemon zest
1 tsp. vanilla
1 1/4 c. ground almonds,
   blanched or unblanched

1 1/4 c. flour
1/2 tsp. ground cinnamon
1/4 tsp. ground cloves
1/2 tsp. salt
2/3 c. raspberry preserves
1 c. fresh raspberries (opt.)

Preheat oven to 350°.

Cream butter and sugar together. Add egg plus yolk, lemon zest, and vanilla; mix well. Sift flour and spices, and add ground almonds to mixture, blending thoroughly. Use a removable bottom pan and spray with vegetable spray. Press 2/3 of the dough on the bottom and 1/2-inch up the sides. Spread with raspberry preserves. On a floured cloth, use hands to roll out a piece from the remaining dough about 1-inch wide, 1/4-inch thick, and long enough to go around the outside edge of the crust over the preserves. With the same thickness of dough, make lattice pieces and place on center over raspberries. Brush dough with egg white. Bake until brown, about 40 minutes.

Time: 40 to 45 minutes
Temperature: 350°
Servings: 12

Janet Matwiyoff   *Albuquerque*

Chocolate Raspberry Brownie Torte

2 oz. unsweetened chocolate, chopped
1 stick (1/2 c.) unsalted butter, cut into pieces
2/3 c. all-purpose flour
1/4 tsp. salt
1/2 tsp. double-acting baking powder
2 lg. eggs
1/2 c. granulated sugar

1/2 c. seedless raspberry jam
2 tsp. Eau-de-Vie de Framboise (raspberry brandy)
1 oz. semisweet chocolate, chopped
Confectioners' sugar for sifting over the torte
Chocolate ice cream, as an accompaniment, if desired

In the top of a double boiler, over barely simmering water, melt unsweetened chocolate with butter. Stir until the mixture is smooth. In a small bowl, combine flour, salt, and baking powder. In another bowl, whisk together eggs, granulated sugar, jam, Eau-de-Vie de Framboise, semisweet chocolate, and melted chocolate mixture. Whisk in flour mixture.

Line a buttered 9-inch round pan with a round of wax paper. Butter the paper. Pour the batter into the pan. Bake the torte in a preheated 350° oven for 25 to 30 minutes, or until a cake tester inserted in the center comes out with crumbs on it. Let the torte cool in the pan on a rack, and remove the paper. Invert the torte onto another rack and let it cool, top side up. Sift confectioners' sugar lightly over the torte. Serve the torte with ice cream, if desired.

Time: 25 to 30 minutes
Temperature: 350°
Servings; 10 to 12

Marilyn Salman, Salman Ranch   *La Cueva*

♥Choco-Berry Mocha Torte

CAKE:

2 T. instant coffee crystals
1/2 c. hot water
1 pkg. lowfat devil's food
   cake mix

3/4 c. cholesterol-free
   egg product, thawed, or
3 egg whites

Note: For altitudes above 3,500 feet: Add 3/4 cup flour to dry cake mix; increase hot water in cake to 1/2 cup. Bake as directed.

Heat oven to 350°. Spray three 9- or 8-inch round cake pans with nonstick cooking spray (or bake layers one at a time).

In small bowl, dissolve 2 tablespoons instant coffee in 1/3 cup hot water. In large bowl, combine cake mix, 1 cup water, egg product, and coffee mixture at low speed until moistened. Beat 2 minutes at high speed. Pour into spray-coated pans. Bake at 350° for 13 to 18 minutes, or until toothpick inserted in center comes out clean. Cool 15 minutes. Remove from pans.

FILLING:

4 1/2 tsp. amaretto, if desired
1/2 c. raspberry spreadable
   fruit or jam

1/2 c. sliced almonds

Prick cake layers with a fork. Sprinkle each with 1 1/2 teaspoons amaretto. Cool completely. Place one layer, amaretto-side up, on serving plate. Spread with 1/4 cup spreadable fruit and sprinkle with 1/4 cup sliced almonds. Repeat with second layer, spreadable fruit and almonds. Top with remaining cake layer.

TOPPING:

4 1/2 tsp. instant coffee
   crystals
1 tsp. hot water
1 (12 oz.) ctn. frozen light
   whipped topping, thawed

1/2 c. sliced almonds
1 1/2 c. fresh raspberries or
   1 1/2 c. frozen raspberries

In small bowl, dissolve 4 1/2 teaspoons instant coffee in 1 tablespoon hot water. Fold into whipped topping until well blended. Reserve 1 to 1 1/2 cups whipped mixture; set aside. Frost sides and top of cake with remaining whipped mixture. Sprinkle top with 1/2 cup sliced almonds. Pipe or spoon reserved whipped mixture

Continued on following page.

Continued from preceding page.

across top of cake in spoke fashion. Refrigerate 2 hours before serving.

Just before serving, place raspberries in a circle near outer edge of top of cake, around bottom edge of cake, and in a small cluster in center of cake. Serve immediately. Store in refrigerator.

Temperature: 350°
Time: 13 to 18 minutes
Servings: 12 to 16

Joy Kittrel   *Albuquerque*

Albuquerque's Joy Kitrell was a finalist in the 1992 Pillsbury Bake-Off contest with this gorgeous, low-fat dessert.

Dessert Sauces

Raspberry Melba Sauce

1 (10 oz.) pkg. frozen
   raspberries, thawed
3/4 c. currant jelly

1 T. cornstarch
1 T. cold water
1 T. Grand Marnier

Strain thawed berries through a sieve to attain 3/4 cup juice. Combine juice and jelly in a small saucepan. Bring to a boil. Combine cornstarch and water; add to syrup. Stir constantly with a whisk until sauce is clear and thick. Remove from heat and stir in Grand Marnier. Cool.

Servings: 4

Delicious with puddings, ice cream, angel food cake, or over fruit salad.

Ilene Karlsson   *Albuquerque*

Royal Raspberry Sauce

1 (10 oz.) pkg. frozen
   raspberries, thawed &
   drained, or 1 1/2 c. fresh
   raspberries

3 T. powdered sugar
1 T. kirsch, Triple Sec
   or orange juice

Purée raspberries in blender or processor until smooth. Put in medium-size bowl. Sieve out seeds, if desired. Add sugar and kirsch. Chill.

Yield: 1 cup

Note: Can be used over vanilla ice cream or yogurt.

Gerry Mlynek   *Albuquerque*

Gerry is an Albuquerque visual artist who is a member of the Very Special Arts exhibit committee.

Fresh Raspberries with Grand Marnier Cream

1 c. whole milk
1 c. heavy cream
1/2 tsp. vanilla extract
4 lg. egg yolks

1/2 c. sugar
1/4 c. Grand Marnier liqueur
1 qt. raspberries (or
   strawberries, cut into
   bite-size pieces)

In top of double boiler, scald milk, cream, and vanilla. In small bowl, beat egg yolks and sugar until light yellow in color. Add egg mixture to milk mixture very slowly, stirring constantly, over low heat until sauce thickens. Stir in liqueur. Pour into a lidded jar and refrigerate. Can be made a week in advance. To serve, bring sauce to room temperature and mix with berries.

Servings: 6 to 8

For an impressive dessert, serve in parfait glasses with alternating layers of frozen yogurt and Grand Marnier Cream mixed with raspberries, and topped with whipped cream and berry garnish.

Nadyne Bicknell   *Albuquerque*

Brandied Raspberries

4 qt. ripe raspberries   2 c. water
2 c. sugar   Fine brandy

Make a thick syrup of equal parts sugar and water. Allow 1/2 cup sugar and 1/2 cup water for every quart of raspberries. Sample brandy, checking for smooth character and light taste. Simmer the raspberries in the syrup for 3 minutes. Taste test brandy and make sure it is at room temperature. Drain raspberries and place in sterile jar (sterilize in advance). Double-check brandy by mouth for correct proof. Pour over each jar, 4 to 6 or 8 or more tablespooners of randy. Resample burandy for taste and character. Purr the styrup over the froot, fillin the chars to the brim. Measure 1/2 cup brandie into measuring kup. Drink immejatly. Seal and process jarrs in boiling wawa for 15 minutes or moor. Quality chek remaning brandee (opin nu boddle if neceshary). Store rasburies in cool dry place 3 mons b4 youzing. Finnish left'over bandy wild waiting.

Raspberries will keep forever. Uwill2.

Bruce Cline   *Albuquerque*

Bruce is a past Board President of Very Special Arts New Mexico. This is his ORIGINAL RECIPE and should be tested in the privacy of your home. Warning: do not drink and drive!

❖

Maggie On Growing Raspberries
The Raspberry Sage says that water is the most important part of growing great raspberries. She uses a drip system and floods the ditches between the rows, especially during thirsty times like blooming or harvesting.

Candy Desserts

Chocolate Raspberry Truffles

1/2 c. heavy cream
1/2 oz. semisweet chocolate, chopped fine
1/2 stick (1/4 c.) unsalted butter, cut into bits & softened
1/2 c. seedless red raspberry jam

2 T. Chambord (black raspberry liqueur), or to taste
Pinch of salt
1/2 c. sifted unsweetened cocoa powder for coating truffles

In a saucepan, bring the cream just to a boil over moderate heat. Remove the pan from the heat. Add the chocolate, stirring constantly. Stir the mixture until the chocolate is melted completely and the mixture is smooth. Let the mixture cool slightly. Add the butter, bit by bit, while stirring. Stir the mixture until it is smooth.

Stir in the jam, the Chambord, and the salt. Transfer the mixture to a bowl and chill it, covered, for 4 hours, or until it is firm. Form the truffles by rolling heaping teaspoons of the mixture into balls. Roll the balls in the cocoa powder.

Chill the truffles on a baking sheet lined with wax paper for 1 hour, or until firm. The truffles will keep in an airtight container, chilled, for 2 weeks.

Yield; 40 truffles

Carolyn Tinker   *Albuquerque*

Carolyn Tinker was the Director of Public Affairs at the University of New Mexico Medical School. She is now associate director of development for UNM.

I Made These!
Raspberry Candies

This recipe is designed for kids to do with their parents. My children and I make candy often. I was quite surprised the first time we did this at the Specialty Shop in Albuquerque. It's easy, fun, and kids feel very proud of the final product.

What you will need:

• Plastic candy molds. You can buy these at large craft stores or cake decorating shops.
• Meltaway candy disks.
• Fresh raspberries (just a small container).

Put the meltaway candy in a microwavable container and melt it on a low setting.

Chop the raspberries into small pieces. Fold the raspberry pieces into the melted candy.

Spoon the mixture into the molds. Grab the edges of the mold and tap it ten times on the table. Put the molds in the refrigerator for 10 minutes, and then turn the molds over onto a plate. TAA-DAA!

Don't worry if kids don't keep all the candy in the mold. The candy will still come out great. They can also dip potato chips, pretzels, peeled apple slices, Oreo and animal cookies, and berries in the candy. Candy sprinkles can be added to make things even more festive! Have fun and enjoy time together.

Deanna Sauceda   *Albuquerque*

Deanna is a news anchor at the CBS affiliate, Channel 13. She received the 1993 YWCA Woman of the Year award for her excellence in news reporting.

Untitled (Tempera)
Marc Frye
Apprentice Artist at ENABLED Art Center,
Albuquerque

Chefs & Restaurants

Andrea and Dennis are with the Assets Grille and Brewing Co. in Albuquerque. The restaurant is known for the gourmet pizzas from the oakwood-fired pizza oven and for having Albuquerque's first microbrewery.

Pecan Crust Rack of Lamb

2 c. finely chopped pecans
1/2 c. bread crumbs
1 tsp. chopped sage
1/4 c. olive oil

Salt
Pepper
1 rack of lamb
1/2 c. Dijon mustard

Preheat oven to 400°. Combine bread crumbs, pecans, salt, pepper, sage, and olive oil. Cut lamb into 4 ribs per person. Coat lamb liberally in Dijon mustard, and dredge in pecan mixture. Place in a roasting pan. Bake in oven for 6 minutes, or until medium rare.

Time: 6 to 8 minutes
Temperature: 400°
Servings: 2

Dennis Apodaca, Assets Grille   *Albuquerque*

Raspberry White Chocolate Crème Brûlee

24 oz. raspberries
1 1/4 c. sugar
4 tsp. Chambord
10 egg yolks
4 c. heavy cream

1/2 tsp. vanilla
6 oz. good quality white
    chocolate
6 tsp. sugar

Toss berries with 1/3 cup sugar and Chambord; divide among twelve 3/4-cup ramekins.

Whisk egg yolks and 1/2 remaining sugar together in bowl. In medium saucepan, bring cream and remaining sugar to simmer. Reduce heat to low. Gradually add chopped chocolate to cream mixture and whisk until smooth. Gradually add hot cream mixture to yolk mixture. Mix in vanilla. Ladle into cups.

Place cups in large baking pan and fill with enough water to go halfway up sides of cups. Bake until they are set in center, about 1 hour. Remove from water; cover and refrigerate overnight.

Before serving, sprinkle 1/2 teaspoon sugar over each one and broil until sugar caramelizes, about 2 minutes.

Time: 1 hour
Temperature: 350°
Servings: 12

Andrea Yablon-Krause, Assets Grille   *Albuquerque*

Daniel Baca is a chef at La Posada which is located in downtown Albuquerque. The well preserved building is on the National Historic Register. Chef Baca was responsible for the first Raspberry Festival brunch that featured twenty-five food items, all containing raspberries. This recipe was enjoyed in the 1990 Raspberry Festival.

Raspberry Cinnamon Rolls

SWEET DOUGH MIX:

1/2 c. sugar	1 1/2 c. warm water
1 T. salt	1 c. milk
7 c. flour	2 eggs
1 pkg. dry yeast	1/2 c. shortening

Mix sugar, salt, and flour. Mix in yeast with warm water. Beat together milk, eggs, and shortening. Combine everything together and place in a stainless steel mixing bowl. Cover with a damp towel and let rise until mixture doubles in size. Cut in 4 equal parts; roll out. Brush with butter and raspberry preserves. Sprinkle brown sugar and cinnamon. Roll dough up and slice. Place on sheet pan. Press rolls down a bit and bake 20 to 30 minutes at 350°.

RASPBERRY ICING;

1 lb. powdered sugar	1/4 c. raspberry jam
1/4 c. coffee	

Mix ingredients together and pour over cinnamon rolls.

Temperature: 350°
Time: 20 to 30 minutes
Servings: 20 (3-ounce) rolls

Daniel Baca, La Posada   *Albuquerque*

Ethel and Sam Ballen are owners of La Fonda hotel. La Fonda is located on Santa Fe's historic Plaza. There has been a fonda, or inn, on the present site since Santa Fe was founded in 1610. It has been known as "the inn at the end of the Santa Fe Trail". The Ballens were pleased to share their private recipes with our readers.

Raspberry Duck Won Tons

FILLING:

1 whole duck (approx. 4 1/2 to 5 1/2 lb.)	1 T. ginger, finely minced
	Zest of 1 orange
1 c. orange juice	1/2 to 1 c. piñon nuts,
1 T. garlic powder	roasted & finely diced
1 T. dried ginger	1 c. scallions, finely julienned
1 clove garlic, finely minced	(green & white parts)
	1 c. fresh raspberries

Pick and clean (and singe if necessary) duck. Dry with paper toweling and rub with salt and white pepper. Set duck on rack in roasting pan; add 1 cup orange juice around duck. Sprinkle with garlic powder and dried ginger.

Roast at 450° for 20 minutes. Reduce heat to 350° and cover pan with lid. Continue to roast, approximately 15 minutes per pound. Remove from oven and allow to cool.

Debone meat and finely shred. Place in bowl with garlic clove, ginger, orange zest, piñons, and scallions. Gently fold in the raspberries. Set aside.

Time and Temperature: 20 minutes at 450°; 1 to 1 1/2 hours at 350°.

WON TONS:

1 pkg. purchased won ton skins	1 to 2 T. water
1 egg	

Cut pastry in quarters. Brush skin with egg wash made from the egg and water. Place 1/4 to 1/3 ounce filling in center of each won ton. Connect edge by folding or pinching. Place prepared won tons in freezer for at least 1 hour. (Won tons can be kept for up to 3 months.)

Continued on following page.

Continued from preceding page.

When ready to serve, fry in 450° deep fat for 5 to 8 minutes. (The won tons should be dropped into hot oil when still frozen, in order to retain their shape. Since the filling is precooked, the frying process needs to firm the outer skin and warm the entire won ton through. If the won ton is not frozen before frying, it will often lose its shape when placed in hot fat.)

Time: 5 to 8 minutes
Temperature: 450°
Yield: 20 to 24 won tons

Ethel and Sam Ballen, La Fonda   *Santa Fe*

Raspberry Walnut Vinaigrette Salad

SALAD:

2 heads Boston Bibb lettuce	4 to 6 oz. walnuts
6 heads baby Red Romaine	12 mushrooms
lettuce	12 black olives, pitted
2 tangerines	1 pt. fresh raspberries

DRESSING:

12 oz. walnut oil	1 tsp. sugar
4 oz. raspberry-flavored wine	1 bay leaf
vinegar	

Using a wire whisk, mix walnut oil, raspberry vinegar, and sugar well. Add 1 bay leaf. Let stand overnight. Mix well before serving.

Clean Boston Bibb and baby Red Romaine. Line Red Romaine around plate. Place Boston Bibb atop. Toast walnuts in oven. Arrange tangerine segments, walnuts, mushrooms, black olives, and raspberries onto lettuce. Top with dressing.

Servings: 6 to 8

Ethel and Sam Ballen, La Fonda   *Santa Fe*

Jean Bernstein is one of the owners of the very popular Double Rainbow Bakery and Cafe on Central Avenue in Albuquerque. Their bakery items are constantly voted one of the city's favorites.

Raspberry Pound Cake

1 lb. unsalted butter,
    softened
3 c. white sugar
6 whole eggs
4 c. white flour
1 T. baking powder
1/2 tsp. salt
1 c. milk

2 tsp. lemon extract
Grated rind of 1 lemon (juice
    the lemon; hold juice in
    reserve)
2 c. fresh raspberries, plus
    raspberries for garnish
1 c. powdered sugar

Cream butter and sugar together. Add eggs, one at a time. Beat until combined. Sift flour, salt, and baking powder together. Add about 1/3 of the dry ingredients to sugar/egg mixture. Mix until just combined. Add 1/2 of the milk and the lemon extract. Mix until combined. Add 1/3 of the flour mixture and so on, until all ingredients are mixed in. Take care not to overmix or cake may collapse. Add lemon rind. Carefully fold in the raspberries. Fold into an oiled and floured tube or bundt pan (large). Bake at 350° for about an hour. A tester should come out clean. Cool and top with a mixture of powdered sugar and lemon juice, beating until it is spreadable. Top with fresh raspberries.

Time: 1 hour
Temperature: 350°
Servings: 12 to 18

*Jean Bernstein, Double Rainbow
Bakery & Cafe*   *Albuquerque*

Growing Raspberries in New Mexico
The most popular raspberry in New Mexico is "Heritage". This is an everbearing real raspberry which produces berries in the fall on the terminal ends of canes produced in the spring and summer of the same year.

Dixie Burch is the General Manager of the Petroleum Club in downtown Albuquerque. The restaurant is a beautiful spot from which to watch the city lights and breathtaking sunsets.

Shrimp and Raspberry Salad with Green Beans

2 c. thin, tender green beans
2 lb. med.-sized shrimp, cooked
5 T. snipped, fresh chives
Grated zest of 1 med.-sized orange

1/2 tsp. freshly ground black pepper
1 c. fresh raspberries
1 bunch watercress, stems removed

Blanch the green beans in boiling water until bright green and just tender, about 1 minute. Drain and drop into ice water to cool. Drain and pat dry. Toss the shrimp and green beans together in a large bowl. Add 4 tablespoons of the chives, the orange zest, and pepper; toss gently.

VINAIGRETTE:
1/3 c. raspberry vinegar
1 tsp. Dijon-style mustard

Salt & freshly ground black pepper to taste
1/2 c. olive oil

Whisk the vinegar and mustard together in a small bowl. Season to taste with salt and pepper. Gradually whip in the oil until thickened.

Pour 3/4 cup of the vinaigrette over the shrimp salad and toss to coat. Add half the raspberries and very gently toss to combine. Arrange the watercress on a serving platter and mound the salad in the center. Garnish with the remaining 1 tablespoon chives and remaining raspberries.

Servings: 6

Dixie Burch, Petroleum Club   *Albuquerque*

Susan Coyle is a chef with the Hyatt Regency Hotel in downtown Albuquerque. These recipes were used in the 1990 Raspberry Festival and included in the Festival's brochure.

Raspberry Brownies

BROWNIES:

1 c. unsalted butter, room
   temperature
1 1/4 c. granulated sugar
1/2 c. firmly packed brown
   sugar
4 lg. eggs
1/2 c. unsweetened cocoa
   powder

1 T framboise eau-de-vie
   (clear raspberry brandy)
   or brandy
1 tsp. vanilla extract
1/4 tsp. salt
1 1/4 c. unbleached all-
   purpose flour
1/2 pt. fresh raspberries

Preheat oven to 325°. Grease a 9x13-inch pan. Beat butter and sugars in large bowl until fluffy. Add eggs, one at a time, beating well after each addition. Stir in cocoa, brandy, vanilla, and salt. Gently mix in flour. Pour batter into preheated pan. Sprinkle raspberries evenly over batter. Bake until tester comes out clean when inserted, about 30 minutes. Cool completely.

GLAZE:

4 oz. semisweet chocolate,
   chopped
2 T. framboise eau-de-vie
   (clear raspberry brandy) or
   brandy

2 T. hot water

Combine chocolate, brandy, and water in double boiler. Melt until smooth. Cool slightly.

Cut brownies; sprinkle with powdered sugar. Use fork to drizzle glaze over brownies. Let stand at room temperature until glaze sets.

Yield: 32 bars

Susan Coyle, Hyatt Regency Hotel   *Albuquerque*

White Chocolate Raspberry Tart

CRUST:

3/4 c. cake flour
3/4 c. all-purpose flour
1/4 c. granulated sugar
1/2 c. chilled, unsalted butter,
   cut into pieces

1 egg yolk
1 T. whipping cream
2 T. cold water

Mix flours and sugar in large bowl. Add butter; cut in until it resembles coarse meal. Beat together egg yolk and cream; add to flour mixture. Stir until dough comes together, adding water if necessary. Gather dough into ball; flatten into dish. Cover with plastic, and refrigerate for at least 30 minutes. Roll out dough 1/8-inch thick. Place in 9-inch tart pan with removable bottom. Trim and finish edges. Refrigerate for at least 30 minutes. Preheat oven to 350°. Line pastry with foil or parchment paper. Fill with dry beans or pie weights and bake 15 minutes. Remove beans and bake another 15 minutes to brown crust. Cool completely on wire rack.

FILLING:

12 oz. white chocolate
   (imported), chopped or
   grated
1/2 c. hot, heavy cream

1/4 c. unsalted butter, room
   temperature
2 c. fresh raspberries, or
   unsweetened frozen
   berries, thawed & drained

Melt white chocolate in double boiler; stir until smooth. Mix in cream and butter. (If you have trouble mixing chocolate until smooth, use electric mixer.) Place raspberries evenly in baked, cooled tart shell. Pour chocolate over raspberries. Refrigerate until firm, about 1 hour. Let stand at room temperature for about 1 hour before serving. Can be made 1 day in advance.

Time: 30 minutes
Temperature: 350°
Servings: 6 to 8

Susan Coyle, Hyatt Regency Hotel   *Albuquerque*

Connie Dempsey is the owner of La Jara Creek Ranch Retreat, located on 70 acres near the Jemez National Forest. The retreat is the perfect place for rest and relaxation. Hiking trails, hot tubs, saunas, and wholesome and delicious meals are available.

Cold Raspberry Soufflé

1/3 c. (2 env.) unflavored
   gelatin
1/3 c. orange juice
1/3 c. lemon juice
4 c. raspberries, rinsed &
   drained

6 lg. egg whites
1 c. sugar
1 1/2 c. heavy cream,
   whipped to hold soft
   peaks

In a 2-cup saucepan, mix gelatin with orange and lemon juices until liquid is absorbed. Stir on medium heat until melted. Purée raspberries in a blender or food processor. Rub purée through a fine strainer into bowl; discard seeds. Add gelatin mixture. Chill, stirring often, until mixture barely thickens, 10 to 15 minutes.

Whip egg whites on high speed until foamy. Slowly add sugar until soft peaks form. Fold whites and whipped cream into purée. Make a 3-inch-wide foil collar on the rim of a 6-cup soufflé dish. Pour into mixture; cover and chill until firm, 3 hours or overnight. Discard foil and serve.

Servings: 10 for dessert; 8 for luncheon

To serve for dessert, add cookies on the side. To serve for luncheon, serve with favorite finger sandwiches or banana nut bread and green salad.

*Connie Dempsey, La Jara Creek
Ranch Retreat*   *La Jara*

Beauregard Detterman Catering is well-known in Albuquerque, especially for his unusual appetizers and exquisite desserts. He is presently producing his own TV interview show called **Entertaining From The Source.**

Sweet Potato Pancakes

1 c. grated sweet potato	Salt & pepper to taste
1 c. grated zucchini	Juice of 1 full lemon
1 c. grated white potato	1/4 c. chopped chives
1 c. Parmesan cheese	1/4 c. chopped parsley
1/3 c. flour	1/4 c. heavy cream

Place grated potatoes in a colander over a bowl. Add salt and pepper. Let stand for 15 minutes. Rinse and squeeze out excess water. Combine other ingredients; mix well and add potato mixture. Drop by tablespoon and sauté in butter or olive oil in heavy skillet until golden brown. Serve immediately, topped with sour cream and raspberry sauce.

SAUCE:

1 c. fresh raspberries	1/4 c. chopped cilantro
1/8 c. balsamic vinegar	1 c. sour cream

Mix raspberries, vinegar and herbs together. Spoon over sour cream-topped pancakes.

Servings: 8

Serve with crisp lettuce salad with fresh fennel.

Beauregard Detterman   *Albuquerque*

One of our committee members, Bobbie Engle, met the Eatons while staying at a bed and breakfast in Santa Fe. Monika was born in Germany and grew up in her parents' cafe, called Stadtcafe, located in Laneensbold. We are delighted Monika is sharing one of her family recipes with us.

Raspberry Tea Bread

1 (10 or 12 oz.) pkg. frozen
    raspberries in light syrup,
    thawed
2 eggs
1/2 c. + 2 T. safflower or
    canola oil

1 c. sugar
1 1/2 c. unbleached white
    flour
1 tsp. ground cinnamon
1 tsp. baking soda

Preheat oven to 350°.

Purée the raspberries along with their syrup in the food processor (fitted with a metal blade) until smooth. Strain and discard the seeds.

Place the eggs, oil and sugar in the bowl of an electric mixer. Mix at medium speed for about 3 minutes. Add the raspberry purée and blend well. Add the flour, cinnamon, and baking soda; mix the batter for about 1 minute at low speed. Scrape the dough into a buttered 9x5-inch loaf pan. Bake until a toothpick inserted in the center comes out clean, about 55 to 60 minutes. Cool for 30 minutes. Remove from pan and cool completely on a wire rack. Wrap tightly in plastic wrap.

Temperature: 350°
Time: 55 to 60 minutes
Yield: 1 loaf

This bread will keep up to 2 weeks in the refrigerator, or it can be frozen for 2 months. It is great served with cream cheese on the side.

Monika Eaton   *Fort Sill, OK*

Karen Garcia is the Sous Chef at High Noon Restaurant. The building that houses High Noon was built about 1785. It is one of the original structures in historic Old Town. At that time, it housed both a gambling casino and a popular brothel.

Walnut Raspberry Vinaigrette

1 c. fresh or frozen
  raspberries
2 T. sugar
2 T. Chambord or raspberry
  liqueur
1 T. Dijon-style mustard

1 c. raspberry vinegar
3 c. walnut or salad oil
1/4 c. chopped walnuts
Salt & cracked black pepper
  to taste

Purée raspberries with sugar and liqueur in food processor or blender. Strain, reserving juice. Discard seeds.

In a medium bowl, combine raspberry purée, vinegar, and mustard. Using a wire whisk, gradually add oil. Stir in nuts and add salt and pepper to taste.

Yield: 4 cups

This dressing is excellent when served atop butter lettuce accompanied with fresh raspberries, jicama, and assorted fruit.

Karen Garcia   *Albuquerque*

This dessert was submitted for the 1991 Raspberry Festival by Mogens Hansen, chef at Le Cafe Miche. The Cafe serves traditional French and Italian cuisine.

Raspberry Ice Cream with Toasted Hazelnuts

4 oz. frozen or fresh
    raspberries
2 c. water
24 oz. sugar
1 T. vanilla

16 egg yolks
1 pt. heavy cream, whipped
4 c. raspberry liqueur
6 oz. toasted, crushed
    hazelnuts

Boil the raspberries in water; strain. Add sugar and vanilla to purée; boil again. Add yolks and whip until fluffy and cool. Add whipped cream together with hazelnuts and liqueur. Fill in molds and freeze in freezer for 24 hours. This is actually a method called "parfait" (perfect). No ice cream maker is needed.

Servings: 4

Mogens Hansen   *Albuquerque*

William Stowe was the sous chef at the Four Hills Country Club when this recipe of his was used in the 1990 Raspberry Festival.

Raspberry Mousse

1 T. unflavored gelatin
1/2 c. boiling water
1 pt. fresh raspberries

1 c. sugar
4 egg whites
2 c. heavy whipping cream

Dissolve gelatin in boiling water. In blender, purée raspberries, sugar and gelatin, then strain mixture. Beat egg whites to stiff peaks; set aside. Beat whipping cream until very stiff and fold in raspberry mixture. Fold in egg whites. Chill until set.

Servings: 6

William T. Stowe   *Albuquerque*

This soup was submitted for the 1990 Raspberry Festival's recipe brochure. Joyce Jones is a Culinary Instructor at Albuquerque's Technical-Vocational Institute.

Raspberry Wine Fruit Soup

2 (10 oz) pkg. frozen
    raspberries in syrup
2 (11 oz.) cans mandarin
    orange segments
1 c. orange juice

1/2 c. Burgundy wine
2 c. blush chablis wine
1/2 c. lemon juice
1/4 c. quick-cooking tapioca
2 T. kirsch liqueur

Drain juice from raspberries and orange segments into saucepan; set fruit aside. Add orange juice, Burgundy, chablis, lemon juice, and tapioca to saucepan. Heat to full boil, stirring occasionally. Remove from heat and cool 30 minutes. Add kirsch and reserved fruits. Refrigerate. Serve cold.

Servings: 8

Joyce Jones   *Albuquerque*

Maggie on Planting Raspberries
Maggie has successfully transplanted raspberries at most times of the year, but early spring seems best. You'll need a deep pit or trench (18 inches, at least) to which you have added 6 inches of well rotted manure or compost and covered with another 6 inches of potting soil. Plant the bush to its original depth and leave a nice ditch for flood watering. Over the years these ditches will fill with compost and soil.

Sharman is the owner and chef of Magidson's Deli in Albuquerque. The Deli is a favorite meeting place for the Raspberry Festival committees.

Raspberry Spread

1 (8 oz.) pkg. cream cheese
1/4 c. Chambord
1/2 c. ground pecans

2 to 3 T. raspberry preserves
2 to 3 drops concentrated
 lemon juice

Blend all ingredients until smooth.

This is wonderful as a spread on toasted bagels, crackers, party breads, or even fresh fruit.

Sharman Hill   *Albuquerque*

Gypsy Raspberry Brownies

3/4 c. melted butter
1 1/2 c. sugar
2 tsp. vanilla
3 eggs, slightly beaten

3/4 c. flour
1/2 c. unsweetened cocoa
1/2 tsp. baking powder
1/2 tsp. salt

Cream butter, sugar, and vanilla. Beat in eggs. In another bowl, stir together flour, cocoa, baking powder, and salt with fork. Blend dry ingredients into egg mixture. Do not overbeat. Spread batter into ungreased 8-inch square baking pan.

FILLING:
1 (8 oz.) pkg. cream cheese,
 softened
1 egg
1/2 tsp. baking powder

1 T. sugar
1 (12 oz.) jar raspberry
 preserves
Powdered sugar

Combine cream cheese, egg, baking powder, and sugar thoroughly. Swirl (use back of spoon to make trenches) cream cheese and raspberry preserves through chocolate batter before baking. Bake 50 to 60 minutes, until brownie pulls away from edges of pan. Cool completely. Dust with powdered sugar and cut into squares.
Time: 50 to 60 minutes
Temperature: 350°
Yield: 16 (2-inch) squares

Sharman Hill, Magidson's Deli   *Albuquerque*

These recipes were featured at the 1990 and 1991 Raspberry Festivals when William Keller was President of the Albuquerque Chef's Association. He was chef for the Four Hills Country Club. He now owns his own catering firm, Rede to Cater.

Fresh Raspberries with Devonshire Cream

1 tsp. unflavored gelatin, softened in 3/4 c. cold water	1 1/2 tsp. vanilla
1 c. heavy cream	2 (8 oz.) ctn. sour cream
1/2 c. sugar	4 pt. fresh raspberries, washed & drained

Heat gelatin in water until it dissolves. Beat heavy cream, sugar, and vanilla in mixing bowl until it forms soft peaks. Combine sour cream with gelatin and fold into whipped cream. Serve over raspberries.

Servings: 4 to 8

William Keller   *Albuquerque*

Raspberry Wine Poached Pears

6 fresh, ripe Bartlett pears	1/2 c. sugar
3/4 qt. dry red wine	2 oz. amaretto or maraschino liqueur
3/4 c. raspberry jelly or seedless jam	

Peel pears. Cut thin slice from bottom so pears will sit upright when served. Do not core or remove stem. Combine wine, jelly and sugar in pan large enough to hold pears in one layer. Heat, stirring occasionally, until jelly and sugar are dissolved, about 5 minutes. Add pears to wine mixture (pears will float) and bring to a boil. Simmer, covered, turning pears occasionally, until pears are tender, about 20 minutes. Cool in liquid. Remove pears from liquid. Boil liquid over high heat until reduced by half, or until syrup coats the back of a spoon. Add liqueur to hot liquid. Pour over pears and cool to room temperature.

Servings: 6

William Keller   *Albuquerque*

Casa Cordova restaurant is nestled in the Sangre de Cristo Mountains on the road to Taos Ski Valley. The quail, chicken, and lamb served at Casa Cordova is hormone and chemical free. The restaurant is recognized for being both beautiful and unique.

Roasted Quail with Raspberry Sauce

4 quail   2 T. butter, melted

Preheat oven to 350°. Place quail in roasting pan. Baste with melted butter. Roast in oven for 10 to 15 minutes.

SAUCE:

1 c. orange juice	2 T. cornstarch
1/2 c. pineapple juice	1/4 c. cold water
1/2 apple, diced	1 c. fresh raspberries
2 T. brown sugar	4 fresh basil leaves

In medium saucepan, heat orange juice, pineapple juice, diced apples, and brown sugar. Bring to a boil. In small bowl, dissolve cornstarch with water. Slowly add cornstarch to boiling sauce, stirring constantly. Boil for 5 minutes, or until it is the consistency of thin jelly. Turn to low heat. Add raspberries and basil.

Remove quail from oven. (It is done if it is firm under wings.) Pour sauce over quail or serve on side.

Time: 10 to 15 minutes
Temperature: 350°
Servings: 4

Alan K. Kinner   *Taos*

Chef Wolfgang Kramer came to the United States from Cologne, Germany. He is chef at the Inn at Rio Rancho.

Raspberry Pineapple Chicken Salad

1 lb. chicken, cooked & chilled
1 lg. apple
1 c. fresh raspberries
1 c. walnuts, chopped

1 c. canned pineapple tidbits, with juice
1/3 c. celery, diced
1 c. mayonnaise (approx.)
2 T. ketchup
Salt & pepper to taste

Dice chicken. Peel and dice apple. Drain pineapple, reserving the juice. Cook juice until reduced to heavy syrup. Combine juice, mayonnaise, ketchup, salt, and pepper. Add to diced chicken, celery, apple, and raspberries. Combine gently. Chill well.

Servings; 4 to 6

May be served in melon half, fresh pineapple half, avocado half, or on croissants.

Wolfgang Kramer, Inn at Rio Rancho   *Rio Rancho*

Raspberry Bavarian Cream

12 oz. fresh (or frozen) raspberries
5 oz. sugar
Juice of 1/2 lemon

Red food color as needed
1 T. + 1 tsp. unflavored gelatin
1/2 c. hot water
1 3/4 c. heavy cream

Combine raspberries, sugar, lemon juice, and food coloring until smooth. Adjust color. Dissolve gelatin in hot water and add to the raspberry mixture. Whip cream and fold into raspberry mixture. Pour into champagne glasses; chill. Garnish with fresh raspberries.

Servings: 8

Wolfgang Kramer, Inn at Rio Rancho   *Rio Rancho*

Maggie's Raspberry Ranch is a cozy Bed and Breakfast in Albuquerque's North Valley. Ranch may be a slight exaggeration. It occupies about a quarter acre with some 150 feet of raspberry bushes. But, when things are in full production, harvest keeps all hands busy staying ahead of ripening berries. Maggie has quite a collection of raspberry recipes.

Maggie's Breakfast Soup

3 c. water	1/2 c. chocolate-flavored
1/2 tsp. salt	Malt-o-Meal
1/3 c. sugar	1 tsp. butter
	1/2 c. fresh or frozen
	raspberries

Bring water to a brisk boil; add salt and sugar. Lower heat and stir in Malt-o-Meal and butter. Cook over low heat for 10 minutes, stirring frequently. Turn off heat and add 1/2 cup fresh or frozen raspberries. Cover and allow to stand until guests are seated. Stir once around pan to disperse raspberries, but not briskly enough to "break up" delicate berries. Serve with fresh plum juice, toast from homemade bread, and raspberry jam.

Servings: 4

"Many guests who visit my Raspberry Ranch Bed and Breakfast are trying to leave milk and eggs from their meals in order to lower their cholesterol. So, I have invented new ways of enticing them to experience HOT CEREAL. They usually complain, 'I haven't eaten this since I was a kid.' The look of surprise and the pleasure they receive is worth all the groaning before they try it."

Maggie Lilley, Maggie's Raspberry Ranch   *Albuquerque*

Chocolate Swirl Cheesecake
with Raspberry Topping

4 chocolate wafers
2 c. yogurt, drained (nonfat,
    if desired)
1 (8 oz.) pkg. cream cheese
    (nonfat, if desired)
2/3 c. sugar
1/4 c. milk

2 T. flour
2 tsp. vanilla
3 egg whites
1 T. butter or margarine
1 T. cocoa
1 tsp. chocolate extract

Heat oven to 300°. Spray a 9-inch springform pan with nonstick spray. Sprinkle chocolate wafer crumbs on pan bottom. Beat thick yogurt and cheese on medium speed until smooth. Add sugar, milk, flour, vanilla and egg whites. Beat again until smooth, about 2 minutes on medium.

In separate bowl, beat butter, cocoa, and chocolate extract until blended. Carefully spread vanilla batter over crumbs in pan. Spoon chocolate batter onto vanilla batter. Swirl with knife for marbled effect. Bake 1 hour and turn oven off. Leave in oven 30 minutes. Remove to cool. Cover and refrigerate.

RASPBERRY TOPPING (Serve warm or cooled):
1 (10 oz.) pkg. raspberries
1/4 c. sugar

2 T. cornstarch

Add enough water to juice to make 1 1/4 cups. Mix sugar, cornstarch and juice mixture in saucepan. Heat to boiling over medium heat. Stir in raspberries. Boil and stir frequently for 1 minute. Cool. Serve over chilled Chocolate Swirl Cheesecake slice.

Time: 1 hour
Temperature: 300°
Servings: 10 to 12

Maggie Lilley, Maggie's Raspberry Ranch   *Albuquerque*

Deborah Madison is the author of The Greens Cookbook *and* The Savory Way. *She lives in Santa Fe, New Mexico. Deborah was the Greens' founding chef when it opened on San Francisco Bay.*

Avocado and Papaya Salad with Mango-Raspberry Vinaigrette

2 sm. shallots, finely diced
Zest & juice of 2 limes
(about 1/4 c. in all)
1/4 c. light olive oil
Salt to taste

1 mango
1/2 c. raspberries
Balsamic vinegar to taste
1 papaya
2 avocados
1 lg. bunch watercress

Combine the shallots, lime zest, and lime juice in a bowl with the olive oil and 1/4 teaspoon salt. Whisk together and let stand.

Peel the mango over a bowl to catch the juice, then slice. Purée enough mango, with the juice, to measure 1/2 cup. Add it to the mixture above. Crush the berries well in a strainer and force the juice into the bowl with the dressing. Whisk together and season to taste with the balsamic vinegar and more salt, if needed.

Halve and peel both the avocado and the papaya. Slice each half diagonally into pieces about 1/3-inch thick. Arrange the watercress in 4 plates and lay the avocado and papaya over it attractively. Spoon the dressing over the avocado and greens. Serve immediately.

Servings: 4

"The dressing is fruity, pleasantly tart, and with the raspberries and mangos, it is the color of a sunset. This makes quite a special first course salad."

Deborah Madison   *Santa Fe*

Mama Mia's submitted this recipe for the 1991 Raspberry Festival brochure. This Albuquerque restaurant is an art deco bistro serving Italian food with a touch of the Southwest.

Raspberry Zabaglione Puffs

PASTRY:

9 oz. puff pastry dough   9 oz. raspberries
1 beaten egg

Preheat oven to 350°. Roll out the puff pastry dough into a sheet about 1/4-inch thick. Cut 4 disks of about 4-inches in diameter. Cut a hole in the center of each disk so that 4 rings of pastry are obtained. Roll dough out again, to a sheet 1/4-inch thick. Cut 4 more disks the same diameter as the rings. Put the whole disks on a cookie sheet. Place the rings atop the whole disks and brush them with beaten egg. Bake for about 10 minutes.

ZABAGLIONE:

4 egg yolks   4 T. Marsala wine
4 T. sugar

Put the egg yolks in the top pot of a double boiler, off the stove. Add sugar and mix well. Add Marsala wine and place the top of the double boiler over the boiling water, whisking constantly until the zabaglione has thickened and puffed up. Remove from heat. Put the puffs on dishes. Put a layer of raspberries in the center of each disk and top with the hot zabaglione.

Temperature: 350°
Servings: 4

Mama Mia's Restaurant   *Albuquerque*

"The Pink Adobe is Santa Fe's own national trea-sure," according to Sean Driscoll, author of **Glorious Food***. He continues, "Created through one woman's (Rosalea Murphy) genius almost 45 years ago, it embodies the artistic, eclectic spirit of Santa Fe."*

Raspberries Aphrodite

1 qt. raspberries
Sugar (to taste)
1 pt. vanilla ice cream,
  slightly softened

1 c. heavy cream, whipped
5 T. Cointreau

Sugar berries to taste. Place in a serving bowl to chill. Combine ice cream and whipped cream. Add Cointreau. Pour over berries.

Servings: 4

Rosalea Murphy   *Santa Fe*

Prairie Star Restaurant submitted these recipes for the 1990 Raspberry Festival brochure. The restaurant is a rambling adobe mansion located in Bernalillo with a dazzling view of the Sandia Mountains.

Raspberry Cocktail Sauce

1 c. raspberry preserves
2 T. Dijon or Chenois mustard

Prepared horseradish sauce
  to taste

Blend all ingredients.

Servings: 4 to 6

Prairie Star Restaurant   *Bernalillo*

Raspberry Vinaigrette

1/2 c. olive oil
1/2 c. raspberry vinegar (see
 below)
1/2 tsp. salt

Freshly ground black pepper
1 T. crème fraîche (see
 below)

Combine all ingredients in a jar. Shake well.

Yield: 1 cup

RASPBERRY VINEGAR:
4 qt. raspberries, crushed   White vinegar

Place raspberries in a 1-gallon glass container and fill with white vinegar. Let stand for 30 days, then strain.

CRÈME FRAÎCHE:
1 c. heavy cream   1 c. sour cream

Whisk together heavy cream and sour cream. Cover loosely with plastic wrap. Let stand in kitchen overnight. Cover and refrigerate for at least 4 hours.

Prairie Star Restaurant   *Bernalillo*

❖

The Elegant Raspberry
If we had to choose just one favorite berry, it would be the raspberry, the most elegant of all. Raspberries have been cherished for centuries, and they never seem to be abundant or affordable enough to be taken for granted. When the season is at its peak, eat them plain or with a bit of cream. Pure pleasure!

Rosa Rajkovic was executive chef at Albuquerque's Monte Vista Fire Station when, in 1993, she won the People's Choice Award as Albuquerque's favorite chef. This recipe is in Rosa's recent cookbook, **The Monte Vista Fire Station Cookbook.**

Chocolate Ganache Torte with Fresh Raspberries

TORTE LAYER:

8 oz. semisweet chocolate
6 T. unsalted butter

8 lg. eggs, warmed in warm
   water & separated
1/2 c. granulated sugar

Preheat oven to 350°.

Butter and flour a 3-inch deep, 10-inch round cake pan and set aside. Melt chocolate and butter in a bowl over a double boiler; whisk until smooth. Cool the chocolate mixture slightly and add egg yolks, one at a time, whisking well after each addition. Whip egg whites to soft peaks and add the sugar slowly to form stiff, but not dry, peaks. Mix the yolks through the chocolate mixture and gently fold in the whites. Pour into the prepared cake pan.

Bake the cake for 45 minutes to 1 hour. A cake tester should come out clean when inserted. Remove the cake from the oven and allow the cake to stand for 5 minutes. Remove the cake from the pan; cool and refrigerate for at least 20 minutes. As the cake cools, the center should sink, creating a "well" for the raspberries and ganache.

GANACHE MOUSSE FILLING:

6 oz. semisweet chocolate
1 c. heavy cream

1/3 c. Chambord liqueur
1 pt. raspberries

Melt 6 ounces chocolate in a mixing bowl over boiling water. Add 1 cup chilled heavy cream and the Chambord; mix at high speed with a hand whisk until firm. The texture should be like that of a mousse.

Place the cake on a wire rack and fill the "well" with raspberries and top with the ganache mousse filling. Refrigerate until cool and firm.

Continued on following page.

Continued from preceding page.

GANACHE GLAZE:

10 oz. semisweet chocolate	1 1/2 c. heavy cream

Melt chocolate with the cream and whisk until smooth. Pour the ganache glaze over the cake and smooth top and sides with a long metal spatula. Chill the torte until the ganache glaze is set. Use a long serrated knife, warmed under running hot water, to cleanly cut the torte. Be sure to run hot water over the knife after each slice. Additional fresh raspberries and sweetened whipped cream can be used to garnish the slices.

Time: 45 minutes to 1 hour
Temperature: 350°
Servings: 12

Rosa Rajkovic, Monte Vista Fire Station   *Albuquerque*

Carl Fritz, owner of the popular Carl's French Quarter Restaurant in Taos, submitted this delicious and unusual salad dressing for our readers.

Carl's Raspberry Vinaigrette

RASPBERRY VINEGAR:

1/4 c. very ripe raspberries	2 c. raspberry vinegar or red wine vinegar

Blend raspberries and vinegar.
Mix the above blended vinegar with:

2 c. light olive oil	1/4 c. fresh, minced parsley
2 c. light vegetable oil	1 T. salt
1/2 c. Dijon mustard	1 T. pepper
1/4 c. orange marmalade	

Yield: 1 3/4 quarts

Carl Fritz   *Taos*

Chef Tom Fenton and colleague, Matt Di Gregary, who is the pastry chef, opened the Range Cafe in Bernalillo in September, 1992, during the Bernalillo Wine Festival. The first day, they ran out of food before they ran out of customers. Anthony started in the restaurant business when he was 16 and joined The Range staff when he was only 20. They are already expanding the restaurant.

New York Strip with Raspberry Glaze

4 (8 oz.) New York strip steaks   Cracked black pepper

Coat one side of steaks with cracked black pepper. Grill or charbroil as desired.

SAUCE:

1 c. red wine   1 c. fresh raspberries
2 T. minced shallots   Salt
1 1/2 c. veal stock   White pepper
1 T. raspberry vinegar

Combine red wine and shallots in saucepan. Cook until reduced to 1/3. Add raspberry vinegar, veal stock, and 1/2 cup raspberries. Reduce to a glaze. Adjust to taste with salt and white pepper. Strain out cooked raspberries. Add 1/2 cup raspberries and pour over broiled steak.

Servings: 4

Anthony Lucero, The Range Cafe   *Bernalillo*

Grilled Salmon with Raspberry Beurre Blanc

FISH:

4 (7 oz.) salmon filets

Enough heated white wine to make 2 inches in bottom of baking dish

Grill or charbroil filets until seared. Heat wine in baking dish. Add filets and bake at 400° for 10 to 12 minutes. Remove filets from dish and set aside.

SAUCE;

2 T. minced shallots
1 oz. Chambord
1 T. raspberry vinegar
3 1/2 T. softened butter
1 c. fresh raspberries

1/2 c. cream (optional)
1/2 tsp. true maple syrup
Salt
White pepper

Add shallots to white wine in baking dish. Reduce until almost dry. Add Chambord, raspberry vinegar, 1/2 cup fresh raspberries, and maple syrup. Heat. Remove from burner and stir in softened butter. Strain out cooked raspberries. Add reserved 1/2 cup raspberries, plus salt and pepper. Serve sauce over salmon.

Time: 10 to 12 minutes
Servings: 4

Note: A traditional buerre blanc does not use cream. Cream may be used as a stabilizer. It should be added to the white wine-shallot reduction.

Anthony Lucero, The Range Cafe   *Bernalillo*

Chicken Breasts with Raspberry Cream Sauce

2 whole boneless, skinless   2 T. unsalted butter
   chicken breasts (about 2 lb.)

Cut chicken breasts in half. Melt butter in sauté pan. Add breasts. Cook about 2 to 3 minutes on each side. Remove and set aside.

SAUCE:
1/4 c. diced onions   1/4 c. heavy cream
4 T. raspberry vinegar   18 fresh raspberries
1/4 c. chicken broth

In same pan, add onion. Cover pan over low heat. Cook until tender. Add vinegar. Raise heat and cook until vinegar is reduced to a syrup. Add chicken broth and cream. Bring sauce up to temperature (heat) about 1 minute. Return chicken to pan and simmer 5 minutes, or until done and sauce is reduced. Remove chicken from pan. Add fresh raspberries to sauce. Do not stir. Pour sauce over chicken.

Servings: 4

Tom Fenton, The Range Cafe   *Bernalillo*

Champberry Sorbet

3 qt. fresh raspberries   4 c. sugar
1 bottle champagne   1/4 c. freshly squeezed
                                  lemon juice

Combine all ingredients and cook over medium heat, stirring frequently, approximately 15 to 20 minutes. Purée and strain to remove seeds. Refrigerate until completely cool. Process in ice cream maker as per directions. (This mixture must be cooked long enough to dissipate the carbonation from the champagne or you will have exploding berries when you purée!)

Servings: 12

Matt DiGregary, The Range Cafe   *Bernalillo*

This recipe comes from Walter Burke Catering in Santa Fe, New Mexico. Walter Burke assisted with the 1991 Native American Very Special Arts Festival.

Caramelized Vidalias with Raspberries

1 pt. raspberries	4 T. balsamic vinegar
2 Vidalia onions	Freshly ground black
8 oz. arugula	pepper (optional)

Slice onions into 4 slices each (3/8-inch thick). Grill until translucent. Arrange warm onion slices on arugula. Scatter raspberries over onions. Drizzle with balsamic vinegar and freshly ground black pepper (optional).

Servings: 4

Chef Roland Richter *Santa Fe*

Wild Oats serves this popular dish in their Albuquerque store. Thane Kenny from Wild Oats was kind enough to share the recipe with us.

Raspberry Chicken Sauté

4 chicken breast halves,	1 T. canola oil
skinned & boned	2 T. raspberry vinegar
1/4 c. dry white wine	1 c. fresh raspberries

Heat oil in a large skillet and sauté the chicken until lightly browned on each side and cooked throughout. Remove the chicken to a platter and keep warm. Add remaining ingredients to the skillet and cook on high heat until the sauce thickens slightly. Pour the sauce over the warm chicken and serve.

Servings: 4

Wild Oats Community Market *Albuquerque and Santa Fe*

James Roger and Flores Roessler, of Olde Tymer's Cafe, a favorite for its sports bar atmosphere, submitted this recipe for the 1991 Raspberry Festival.

Roast Turkey with Raspberry Orange Sauce

1 (4 lb.) boneless turkey breast	2 carrots, cut into chunks
2 stalks celery, cut into chunks	White & red pepper to taste
1 med. white onion, cut into chunks	

Heat oven to 350°. Place turkey in roasting pan on a rack. Add 1 cup water, celery, onion, and carrots. Sprinkle white and red pepper to taste. Cover roasting pan with foil and place in preheated oven. After 40 minutes, insert meat thermometer; remove foil. Baste turkey breasts with the juices and allow to brown. When the temperature reaches 160°, remove turkey and set aside.

RASPBERRY ORANGE SAUCE:

1 1/2 c. fresh or frozen raspberries	1/4 c. freshly squeezed orange juice
1/4 c. sugar	1/4 c. piñon nuts, chopped
1 T. butter	

Purée the raspberries and sugar in a food processor. Strain out the seeds with a cheesecloth. In a skillet, heat the butter over medium heat; add orange juice slowly with a whisk. When this reaches a smooth consistency, add raspberry juice and chopped piñon nuts. Slice roasted turkey breasts and ladle raspberry sauce over the slices.

Time: 40 minutes
Temperature: 350°
Servings: 6 to 8

James Roger and Flores Roessler   *Albuquerque*

Santacafe has been named 3 times by Conde-Nast Traveler as one of America's Top 50 Restaurants. Gourmet magazine printed this recipe after its editor, Gail Zweigenthal, visited Santacafe in 1992. Bobby Morean from Santacafe has given us permission to use this exceptional recipe.

Santacafe's White Chocolate Raspberry Cheesecake

CRUST:

2 c. graham cracker crumbs	1/4 c. clarified butter in its
1 c. slivered, blanched almonds	liquid, unchilled form
	(see below)

In the food processor, blend the graham cracker crumbs and the almonds until the almonds are ground fine. Add the butter and combine the mixture well. Press the mixture onto the bottom and 2/3 of the way up the side of a 10-inch springform pan.

Clarified Butter: Place 1 pound butter in at least a 2-quart saucepan over low heat. Melt butter 5 to 6 minutes, depending on the heat of the element or gas. Watch carefully. A milky substance will rise in small bubbles until the entire surface is covered with it. Raise the heat a little and this will turn into a foam. Skim this off as it forms. (Keep the skimmings; they can be used to butter baked potatoes.) Remove the skimmed butter from the heat and allow to settle for a couple of minutes. Pour the now clear butter slowly through muslin to remove the sediment that has settled to the bottom of the pan.

Store the clarified butter in a jar in the refrigerator and use as needed.

FILLING:

8 oz. fine quality white chocolate (preferably Callebaut)	4 lg. whole eggs
	2 lg. egg yolks
	2 T. all-purpose flour
4 (8 oz.) pkg. cream cheese, softened	1 tsp. vanilla
	2 pt. raspberries
1/2 c. + 2 T. sugar	

Continued on following page.

Continued from preceding page.

In a metal bowl set over a pan of barely simmering water, melt the chocolate, stirring until it is smooth. Remove the bowl from the heat. In a large bowl, beat the cream cheese until it is light and fluffy. Add the sugar and beat in the whole eggs and the egg yolks, one at a time, beating well after each addition. Beat in the flour and the vanilla. Add the melted chocolate in a slow stream. Beat until the filling is combined well.

To assemble: Scatter the raspberries over the bottom of the crust. Pour the filling over them, and bake the cheesecake in the middle of a preheated 250° oven for 1 hour, or until the top is firm to the touch. Let the cheesecake cool in the pan on a rack. Chill it, covered loosely, overnight, and remove the side of the pan.

Time: 1 hour
Temperature: 250°
Servings: 10

Santacafe   *Santa Fe*

Growing Raspberries in New Mexico
Raspberries that thrive in acid soils in the East and Northeast can also do well in New Mexico's alkaline soil if they're properly planted. The trick is in the way the plants get started. Raspberries normally are established from bareroot cuttings according to George Dickerson, horticulture specialist with NMSU's Cooperative Extension Service. When these acid loving cuttings get poked down in our alkaline soils, many die. However, the plants that do survive tend to grow like weeds if given plenty of water.

Barbara Shiller is from the Sagebrush Bed and Break-
fast in Corrales. The peaches are grown in Corrales and
she usually picks them herself. She serves this in the
afternoon with iced tea to weary guests who have
returned from their travels.

Raspberry-Peach Torte

1/2 tsp. ground nutmeg	1/2 c. cornstarch
1 tsp. vanilla extract	1/2 tsp. salt
1/2 c. shortening	1 1/2 tsp. double-acting
1 c. (less 2 T.) sugar	baking powder
1 1/8 c. sifted all-purpose	1/4 c. + 1 T. milk
flour	2 lg. eggs, beaten

Combine first 3 ingredients. Gradually blend in sugar. Sift together next 4 ingredients and add to sugar-shortening mixture alternately with milk and eggs. Grease and line bottom of a 9-inch layer cake pan with wax paper. Add batter and spread over bottom to cover evenly. Bake in preheated oven (275°) for 45 minutes. Cool in pan 20 minutes. Turn onto wire rack and remove wax paper at once. Turn torte right side up. Top with Raspberry-Peach Cream Topping. Garnish with remaining sliced peaches and raspberry.

RASPBERRY-PEACH CREAM TOPPING:

1 c. heavy cream	1 c. fresh raspberries
2 T. sugar	1/2 to 1 c. fresh, sliced
1 tsp. vanilla	peaches

Whip heavy cream to soft, stiff peaks. Add 2 tablespoons sugar and 1 teaspoon vanilla. Mix lightly. Fold in 1/2 cup each raspberries and peaches.

Servings: 6 to 8

Note: This recipe is adjusted for altitudes above 3500 feet. For lower altitudes, decrease flour to 1 cup and milk to 1/4 cup. Increase sugar to 1 cup. Bake at 350°. For those who must watch their diets carefully, you can substitute lowfat whipped topping for the whipped cream and omit the sugar and vanilla used in the cream.

Barbara Shiller   *Corrales*

Susan Spring is the pastry chef for Scalo, a fine Northern Italian restaurant located in the Nob Hill area. It is consistently listed as one of the city's top ten restaurants.

Raspberry Tart Scalo

PASTA FROLLA:

1 1/4 c. + 2 T. flour	1 egg yolk
1/4 c. sugar	2 T. heavy cream
1/4 lb. unsalted butter	

Combine flour, sugar and butter in the bowl of a food processor; pulse the machine on and off to combine the ingredients. Mix the yolk and cream together in a small bowl. With the machine running, add the cream mixture and process until the dough begins to pull into a ball.

Lightly flour the ball of dough and roll it out between 2 sheets of plastic wrap. Gently fit it into an 11-inch tart pan with removable bottom. Bake at 350° for 15 to 20 minutes, or until the edges are just beginning to brown; set aside to cool.

CHEESECAKE FILLING:

1/4 lb. unsalted butter	1 tsp. vanilla
3/4 c. sugar	2 eggs
1/2 lb. cream cheese	

Combine all ingredients in the food processor and process until smooth. Pour the filling into the cooled tart shell and bake at 375° for about 30 minutes, or until set. Cool.

TOPPING:

1/3 c. seedless raspberry jam	3 boxes fresh raspberries

Brush the top of the tart with the jam and arrange the raspberries, stem end down, in rows on the top of the tart.

RASPBERRY SAUCE:

1 (10 oz.) pkg. frozen,	1/2 c. sugar
unsweetened raspberries,	1/4 c. water
defrosted	2 T. fresh lemon juice

Continued on following page.

Continued from preceding page.

Purée all ingredients in the food processor and press through a strainer to remove the seeds. Serve wedges of the tart on a plate decorated with a pool of raspberry sauce.

Time: Tart shell: 15 to 20 minutes; Filled tart: 30 minutes
Temperature: Tart shell: 350°; Filled tart: 375°
Servings: 12

Susan Spring   *Albuquerque*

This dessert was submitted by Stephen's Restaurant for the 1991 Raspberry Festival. The owner, Bill Anixter, opened Stephen's when he couldn't find what he thought was a really good American cuisine restaurant.

Stephen's Raspberry Mousse

2 c. red raspberries, cleaned   2 T. cold water
   & crushed   1/4 c. boiling water
1/8 tsp. salt   2 T. lemon juice
3/4 to 1 c. confectioners' sugar   2 c. heavy cream
1 1/2 tsp. gelatin

Stir raspberries, salt, and sugar together. Soak gelatin in cold water and dissolve in boiling water. Cool and add lemon juice; stir into fruit mixture. Chill thoroughly. Whip the heavy cream until thickened, but not stiff. Fold into fruit and gelatin mixture. Spoon into individual glasses for serving. Chill.

Servings: 8

Stephen's Restaurant   *Albuquerque*

El Pinto boasts a tradition of serving authentic New Mexican cuisine for 25 years. Jim and John Thomas continue this tradition and have recently added the Patio Garden.

Raspberry Flan

1/2 c. sugar
2 (10 oz.) pkg. frozen
   raspberries, thawed
1 1/2 c. half & half, scalded
5 eggs

1 egg yolk
3/4 c. sugar
1 tsp. vanilla
Fresh raspberries to garnish

Place a 2-quart baking dish in preheated oven until warm. Heat 1/2 cup sugar in a small saucepan over low heat, stirring constantly, until sugar dissolves and turns golden. Pour melted sugar into the warm baking dish and tilt to coat the bottom and 1/2-inch of sides. Invert baking dish on a plate and let stand to harden sugar.

Press raspberries through a sieve and discard the seeds. Reserve 1 1/4 cups of the stained raspberry liquid. Stir reserved raspberry liquid gradually into egg mixture. Pour into prepared baking dish. Place baking dish in shallow baking pan on oven rack and pour 1/2 inch hot water into baking pan. Bake, uncovered, for about 1 hour and 15 minutes at 350°, or until knife inserted 1 inch from edge comes out clean.

Remove baking dish from water and cool until lukewarm. Cover and refrigerate until cold. To serve, loosen edges with a spatula and invert onto a serving plate. Garnish with fresh raspberries.

Time: 1 hour and 15 minutes
Temperature: 350°
Servings: 8 to 10

Jim and John Thomas, El Pinto Restaurant   *Albuquerque*

Humphrey's Cafe is located in Albuquerque. The Whites own and operate the cafe, as well as the cafe at the Natural History Museum. They are also noted for their catering.

Raspberry Duck

1 whole duck	1 tsp. pickling spice
1 onion	1 orange
3 celery ribs	Salt & white pepper to
2 bay leaves	taste
2 carrots	

Remove viscera from duck and wash thoroughly. Place in large stock pot with onions, celery, bay leaves, carrots, and pickling spice. Cover with cold water. Bring to boil and poach 45 minutes. Remove duck and skim the fat from the top of the water; continue to reduce stock to 2 cups (approximately 2 hours).

Place duck, breast side up, on a roasting rack in a roaster pan. Squeeze the juice of 1 orange over the duck. Sprinkle with salt and white pepper. Place the squeezed orange in the duck and put in a preheated 350° oven. Roast until golden brown. Remove rack and duck from pan. Place pan full of drippings on stove.

Deglaze the pan with the strained stock, being sure to scrape all the drippings from the bottom of the pan.

Add:

1/2 c. raspberry vinegar	1 c. Chambord liqueur
1 pt. fresh raspberries (save	1 tsp. concentrated orange
6 for garnish)	juice

Combine all ingredients. Cook and reduce to one cup. Skim all the fat while the liquid is reducing. Remove all bones, except the leg and wing bone. Place duck on plate and pour the sauce over the duck. Place 3 raspberries on each 1/2 duck. Garnish with a sprig of watercress.

Temperature: 350°
Servings: 2

Annette Cullen-White and James White　　　　　　　　*Albuquerque*

Notes